To Jenn
from
Tom

Tom McNab

Tom has experienced success as an Olympic coach, prize-winning novelist and as the Technical Director of the Oscar-winning *Chariots of Fire*. One of the world's leaders in sport, he has coached international athletes such as Greg Rutherford, the British Olympic Bobsleigh team and England's silver medal-winning squad in Rugby's 1991 World Cup. In that same year, he was awarded the British Coach of the Year. As National Athletics Coach, Tom created many successful initiatives, including the national decathlon programme, which produced Daley Thompson.

Tom has written several best-selling novels, including number one best-seller *Flanagan's Run* and in 1982 won the Scottish Novelist of the Year Award. A commentator for ITV and Channel 4, he has been a freelance journalist for the *The Observer, The Guardian, The Sunday Telegraph, The Times* and *The Independent*.

He has written both radio plays and stage plays. This is his first collection of plays to be published.

www.tommcnab.com

First published in the UK in 2019 by Aurora Metro Publications Ltd.

67 Grove Avenue, Twickenham, TW1 4HX 020 3261 0000

www.aurorametro.com   info@aurorametro.com

Follow us: @aurorametro   facebook.com/AuroraMetroBooks

Foreword © 2019 Jenny Lee

Introduction © 2019 Tom McNab

1936: Berlin © 2019 Tom McNab

Orwell on Jura © 2019 Tom McNab

Whisper in the Heart © 2019 Tom McNab

Front cover image courtesy of Sheila Burnett. It shows Cornelius McCarthy as Jesse Owens in *1936* performed at the Lilian Baylis Studio.

Cover design © 2019 Aurora Metro Publications Ltd.

Production: Peter Fullagar and Cheryl Robson

ISBNs

978-1-912430-11-6 (print)

978-1-912430-12-3 (ebook)

1936:BERLIN

and other plays

by

TOM MCNAB

AURORA METRO BOOKS

CONTENTS

THE PLAYS:

Foreword

I met Tom in 1992, in the BBC when we were rehearsing *Winning*, his play for Radio 4, with Brian Cox. I was struck by the colour and humour in his writing and the ease with which he communicated the world of the play. We became friends, I read *Flanagan's Run*, and from time to time he came to see the work of my theatre company, the ATTIC. My policy was to develop new writing, as well as revive neglected classics, and we were the resident company in Wimbledon Theatre Studio. I think this inspired him to write for theatre. Tom has an encyclopaedic knowledge and is fascinated by history and the lives of great men and women. As a director, I was fascinated by the possibilities and challenges of stage production, and when Tom started to write for the stage, we decided to work in tandem.

His first stage play was *Houdini and Sir Arthur* in 2004. ATTIC Theatre Company commissioned him to write a play about the Home Front and the play that he wrote titled *Dancing In The Dark* went into production in 2005. It premiered at The Clocktower Croydon and toured. ATTIC went on to produce his next play, *1936* in 2008, in the form of a staged radio play. It was performed in London at Tara Arts, New Wimbledon Studio and The Clocktower Croydon. The script was then developed with ATTIC and the full production of *1936* premiered at the Arcola Theatre, London in 2010, to glowing reviews. It was re-mounted at the Lilian Baylis Studio in Sadler's Wells Theatre for the London Olympics in 2012. *Leni-Leni* followed, a play about Leni Riefenstahl, and was produced as a short film, premiering in Berlin and showing at Cannes Film Festival in 2017. *Whisper In the Heart* and *Orwell On Jura* have both had staged rehearsed readings at Trestle Arts Base in St Albans. Tom's latest novel *Ready* was published in 2018.

– Jenny Lee

Introduction

My first career was in sport, as a coach, and I had written many technical and historical books on athletics before moving on to write a novel, *Flanagan's Run* in 1982. At the age of seventy, in the full bloom of youth, having written three radio plays for the BBC, I set upon writing for the theatre. I was a late starter. You might therefore describe me, at eighty-five, as an emerging playwright.

This first collection offers three of my most recent plays, ones which feature some of the major figures of the 20th century, in the worlds of sport, politics and the arts.

1936:Berlin

In the Olympic movement there have frequently been gaps 'twixt precept and practice. Thus it was prior to the 1936 Berlin Olympic Games, because in 1933 Adolf Hitler had embarked upon his persecution of German Jews, and had banned them from all sports clubs, in direct contravention of Olympic rules.

The play follows the attempt by American administrators to boycott the 1936 Berlin Olympic Games. It features the future IOC chairman, Avery Brundage, Jesse Owens, Joseph Goebbels, Leni Riefenstahl and Adolf Hitler.

The story is recounted by an American journalist, William Shirer, and a main character is that great athlete Jesse Owens, who is encouraged to lead a negro boycott of the Games as a response to the persecution of German Jewish sportsmen.

The play explores the gap between Olympic rhetoric and reality and the irony of the USA, a nation in which racism was endemic, attempting to secure an Olympic boycott on racial grounds.

Orwell on Jura

Never let your education interfere with your studies. I have always therefore been a promiscuous reader, and spent much of my youth in

Glasgow libraries. Thus, by the age of 17, I had read most of the essays and novels of George Orwell.

Running through everything that Orwell wrote is the search for truth, a desire for fairness and justice. But I was nevertheless totally unprepared for his final novel, which challenged the very basis of my Scottish education, a total belief in and respect for authority.

My play covers George Orwell's final, stricken days at Barnhill farm on the isle of Jura, completing a dystopian novel called *The Last Man in Europe*. Orwell had a boating accident, arrived seriously ill in Hairmires Hospital, and only the intervention of his editor, Lord Astor, saved his life. For Astor, with the help of Health Minister Aneurin Bevin, managed to secure from the USA a new wonder drug called streptomycin, and this made it possible for Orwell to return to Jura. It enabled him to complete what was to be his final work, a novel now titled *1984*.

Whisper In The Heart

Orson Welles and Leni Riefenstahl never met. In my play, they do, in 1955 in Spain, where a rejected, down at heel Welles has arrived to film an episode for a British television series titled *Around The World With Orson Welles*.

Welles was one of the great wayward geniuses of 20th century arts, excelling as a director, writer and actor in radio, theatre and film. So also, in a different way, was Riefenstahl, though her body of work was much less extensive. Her film *Olympia*, on the 1936 Olympic Games, is considered to be one of the greatest documentaries ever made, and in later life she became an outstanding stills photographer.

In 1960, whilst teaching in Bermuda, I had a brief contact with Riefenstahl, when I tried to purchase a copy of *Olympia*. Alas, her price of £250 was at that point, well beyond my means, but I persuaded the Bermudan government to purchase the film. It was only many years later that I discovered that the money could not have come at a better time for the struggling Riefenstahl.

In the play, at this point in time, both of these great artists have been rejected – Welles by Hollywood, Riefenstahl by the European film industry. Welles' producer Carruthers has suggested to him that, as his Spanish theme is the sport of pelota, then it might be worth bringing on board an expert in sport – Leni Riefenstahl – and Welles agrees.

In their brief fortnight together, the two directors reveal to each other what has brought them to their present pass, and with it certain truths which they must now face if they are to progress.

– Tom McNab

With special thanks to: Jenny Lee, Matt Llewellyn Smith for his tireless research and editing of video footage, Michael Vaughan for his input on the scripts, Caroline Funnell for inspired casting and all the actors who took part in the productions and readings of my work. Thanks also to Pars Pies for their support in kind and the Macnaughtons, Andrew Scott, Alistair Audsley, Mehrdad Garossi, Trevor Newey, Coupers Cars, Austin Trueman Assocs, Elizabeth Uwaifo and Sidley Austin LLP for their financial support.

1936: BERLIN

1936 was first produced by the ATTIC Theatre Company and premiered at the Arcola Theatre, London on 7th April 2010 with the following cast and creative team:

William Shirer	Jim Creighton
Theodore Lewald	Jonathan Battersby
Carl Diem	David Baron
Adolf Hitler	Tim Frances
Joseph Goebbels	Chris Myles
Christine Muller	Josephine Taylor
Leni Riefenstahl	Kate Cook
Avery Brundage	Peter Harding
Judge Jeremiah Mahoney	Jonathan Battersby
Jesse Owens	Rolan Bell
General Charles Sherrill	Tim Frances
Coach Snyder	Jonathan Battersby
Werner March	Peter Harding
Gretel Bergmann	Josephine Taylor
Edwin Bergmann	Peter Harding
Miss Goldstein	Kate Cook
Count Baillet-Latour	David Baron

Other parts were played by members of the cast.

Director	Jenny Lee
Assistant Director	Mel Hillyard
Designer	Kevin Jenkins
Assistant Designer	Jinwoo
Lighting Design	Howard Hudson
Sound Design	Tom Gibbon
Stage Manager	Matt Llewellyn Smith
Casting Director	Caroline Funnell
ATTIC General Manager	Victoria Hibbs

The production was re-mounted at the Lilian Baylis Studio in Sadler's Wells Theatre in August 2012 as part of the Cultural Olympiad.

CHARACTERS
Germany

Theodore Lewald, IOC member, 1936 Olympics organiser.

Carl Diem, Sports historian, 1936 Olympics organiser.

Adolf Hitler, Chancellor of Germany.

Joseph Goebbels, Minister of Propaganda.

Christine Muller, Austrian Olympic fencer.

Werner March, Architect of 1936 Olympic stadium.

Leni Riefenstahl, Actress, film director.

Gretel Bergmann, German high jumper.

Edwin Bergmann, Gretel's father.

America

William Shirer, American journalist.

Avery Brundage, Head of the AAU until 1935. Member of IOC.

General Charles Sherrill, Member of IOC.

Jesse Owens, Olympic athlete.

Coach Larry Snyder, Jesse Owens' coach.

Judge Jeremiah Mahoney, Head of the AAU after Brundage.

England

Miss Goldstein, Athletics coach.

France

Count Henri Baillet-Latour, President of IOC.

A cast of 10 can double roles for Schmidt, newspapermen and women, chairmen etc.

Note

IOC = The International Olympic Committee

AAU = Amateur Athletic Union (America)

Setting

The play begins and ends in the Berlin Olympic Stadium in 1948 at the time of the Berlin Airlift, and flashes back to the events leading up to the Games in 1936.

Scene 1

The 1936 Olympic stadium after the war. It has been used as a place of refuge, and bits of domestic life are scattered around, mixed in with army gear. The lanes of the old running track are still partly visible. There are elements of a high jump stand, an old umpire's chair, canvas chairs and a rough wooden table such as might be found on a sports field or used for military field operations.

SFX The roar of excited crowds, intermixed with a babble of voices, and the distant clanging of the great Olympic Bell.

HITLER *(v/o)* Ich verkunde die spiele Olympique von Berlin als veroffnete. [I now declare the Berlin Olympic Games the eleventh of the modern era, open.]

The roars of the crowd in response, gradually fading as the lights come up on Shirer. In the background, soldiers and civilians come on carrying crates and food parcels to relieve the Berlin blockade. There is a photographer, and a journalist, GIs, German soldiers, and civilians, some checking off the supplies as they come in. The drone of planes is heard.

SHIRER   That was then. This is now. Berlin, December 1948, ten degrees below zero. Day after day, hour after hour, thirteen thousand tons of food and supplies air-lifted in — just to keep alive those same Germans we were bombing the hell out of three short years ago. And Berlin 1936 seems a million miles away to me now, another time, another world. Me, Bill Shirer, I was here right from the start, back in '33, working for the American International News Service and the Olympics, well that was one of my very first assignments. But it had all really begun two years before. Two years before Hitler, before the Nazis came into power. And it all started on May 13th, in the home of the chairman of the German Olympic Committee, Professor Theodore Lewald. With him that day was his friend and colleague, Professor Carl Diem.

Theodore Lewald and Carl Diem sit, silent, at ends of a table, with a telephone in the middle. Suddenly the phone rings, and hesitant, Lewald reaches out and places it to his ear.

LEWALD   Yes... This is Theodore Lewald... yes... thank you very much indeed, Henri. A letter will follow? Thank you, thank you very much indeed, Henri. *(He replaces the telephone, and sits back, clearly moved.)*

DIEM   Well?

LEWALD   That was Count Baillet-Latour, Carl. The chairman of the International Olympic Committee.

DIEM   I know who he is, Theodore. We both know who he is. So are you going to tell me what he SAID?

LEWALD *(stands)* We have done it, Carl. We've done it. We've got the 1936 Olympic Games. They are coming here, to Berlin.

Diem stands and the two men embrace.

Scene 2

SHIRER   Two years later, the first of March 1933, and just eight weeks after Adolf Hitler came to power, Hitler consulted with his Minister of Propaganda.

HITLER *(abrupt)* These Olympic Games, Joseph, is it possible, can we cancel them?

GOEBBELS *(flustered)* Well yes, I should imagine so, Führer. We cancelled them back in 1916.

HITLER   No, it was different then, Joseph. The War. No loss of face back in 1916. So exactly how much did those Americans spend last year, in Los Angeles?

GOEBBELS *(shuffles nervously through his papers)* I have it here, Führer. Nearly three million American dollars.

HITLER   Three million dollars! And how many gold medals did we win in Los Angeles?

Again Goebbels struggles through his notes. He is not in his comfort zone.

GOEBBELS   Just a moment... just a moment. Three gold medals, Führer.

HITLER   Only three! Which sports?

GOEBBELS *(quickly finds what he wants)* Let me see... yes, yes, I have it now, Führer. Weightlifting, rowing and... and... Graeco Roman wrestling.

HITLER   Graeco Roman wrestling! The Third Reich has an army to build, Joseph. Germany will not thank us for spending three million dollars on Graeco Roman wrestling.

GOEBBELS   No, Führer.

HITLER   Your Olympic fellow, this Professor Lewald. Does he know what he is talking about?

GOEBBELS   Theodore Lewald is chairman of our National Olympic Committee. And a member of the International Olympic Committee.

HITLER   You have not quite answered my question.

GOEBBELS   The man is an idealist, Führer.

HITLER   Oh. Men like that often do strange things. Always tempted to do something honourable.

GOEBBELS   Indeed, Führer.

HITLER   And these Olympic committees. Refresh my memory. What was it that Count Bismarck once said... about committees, Joseph?

GOEBBELS *(pleased)* I have it, I have it, Führer. "A group of people individually capable of nothing, and who decide as a group that nothing can be done."

HITLER *(chortling)* Bismarck! Speak to your Professor Lewald, Joseph. Find out exactly what this Olympics of his will involve, and exactly how much they will cost us. Then come back to me on Friday with your recommendations.

GOEBBELS *(dismayed)* Friday? Yes, Führer.

HITLER   And before you go, your idealist sent me this. What is it?

He withdraws a small Olympic flag and holds it up.

GOEBBELS   It is an Olympic flag, Führer.

HITLER   And these five circles?

GOEBBELS   They represent the five continents of the world, bound in unity.

HITLER   Sport and unity? A contradiction in terms, Joseph. A contradiction in terms.

Scene 3

Goebbels sits at his desk, eyes closed, listening to "Siegfried" on his gramophone. There is a knock at the door and an official enters.

GOEBBELS *(peevishly)* Yes?

OFFICIAL   Professor Lewald is here to see you, Reichsminister.

GOEBBELS   Send him in.

OFFICIAL   Yes, Reichsminister. *(to Lewald, outside)* The Minister will see you now.

Lewald enters, carrying a bulky file.

LEWALD *(with a straight arm)* Heil Hitler.

GOEBBELS *(casual bent arm)* Heil Hitler.

Lewald stands stiffly, awkwardly, Goebbels rises and takes the needle from the record and resumes his seat.

LEWALD   You have managed to read my Report, Minister?

GOEBBELS   Yes, Lewald. *(Pause)* I have scrutinised your Olympic Report in great detail.

LEWALD   And the Führer?

GOEBBELS   No, not yet. The Führer is a busy man, Lewald, a very busy man. He has ordered that I should first speak with you and report back to him on Friday.

LEWALD   Friday? I see.

GOEBBELS   No, my dear Lewald, I am not quite certain that you do. You see, if the application for the Olympic Games had been up to the Reichschancellor, then it is highly probable that no bid for the Berlin Olympic Games would have been submitted in the first place.

LEWALD *(deflated)* Oh.

GOEBBELS   Politics is the language of priorities, Lewald. Six million unemployed cannot be gainfully engaged in Graeco Roman wrestling.

LEWALD   So...?

GOEBBELS   So please give me something, something of worth, something of value that I can take with me to the Führer on Friday, Lewald. Preferably on a single sheet of paper.

LEWALD   Is there any particular emphasis you wish me to make, Reichsminister?

GOEBBELS   Yes. First, on no account must you make any mention of Baron de Coubertin.

LEWALD   Yes.

GOEBBELS   Or any reference to the Olympic family. Or legacy. Avoid that.

LEWALD   I see.

GOEBBELS   But, and this is the crux of the matter — justify to me exactly why we should be spending twelve million Reichsmarks on the eleventh Olympic Games. Make your case to me, man, make your case.

Scene 4

SHIRER   Two days later, Goebbels made his weekly visit to the flat of his mistress, Christine Muller.

Goebbels sits with his back, on a bed. Christine appears, in dressing gown.

CHRISTINE   Will that be all you require of me for the day, Reichsminister?

GOEBBELS *(preoccupied)* Yes, Christine... for the moment. Yes.

CHRISTINE   Then, if you have no objection, I'll take a shower.

She turns and enters the shower and it is turned on.

GOEBBELS *(calling after her)* I have a meeting with the Führer on Friday, Christine...

CHRISTINE *(through the noise of the shower)* What? A meeting... a meeting with who?

GOEBBELS   With the Führer. These Olympic Games, Christine...

CHRISTINE *(shouting)* Can't hear a single word of what you are saying, darling.

GOEBBELS   These wretched Olympic Games, Christine. I am at my wits end.

CHRISTINE   Just give me a moment, pussycat. Let me finish my shower first. Then I can offer you my complete attention.

GOEBBELS *(bellowing)* No, woman. I need to speak to you NOW! This is important. Please turn that damn thing off.

The shower is turned off. Christine appears, wrapped in a towel.

CHRISTINE   Pussycat! You ARE in a bother, aren't you?

GOEBBELS *(flustered)* Sport, Christine, sport! You were in Los Angeles at the last Olympics weren't you?

CHRISTINE   Yes. Throw me that towel — it's there across the chair. *(Goebbels throws the towel to her and she catches it)* Yes,

I competed in the foil. *(Dries her face and hair)* Went down to an American girl, in the second round. Now, a year later, I go down on you every Wednesday afternoon. Christine Muller has come on in the world.

GOEBBELS   Christine, perhaps I haven't made myself clear. The Berlin Olympics has now become an issue of national importance. I have to present a paper to the Führer on the Olympics on Friday. And as of this moment, I have nothing, absolutely nothing.

CHRISTINE   Nothing at all? That's not your style.

GOEBBELS   Oh, this Olympic fellow Lewald has given me some stuff, and I have written the usual waffle, thirty-five pages of it, but the Führer, he's got a mind like a razor, he'll cut it to ribbons.

CHRISTINE   But... surely you have all the statistics? *(Goes back in shower to put on dressing gown)*

GOEBBELS   Statistics are like people, Christine. Torture them enough and they'll tell you anything. My Report — here, would you look at it?

CHRISTINE   No thank you, darling. I'd rather not, if you don't mind.

GOEBBELS *(deflated)* Oh!

CHRISTINE *(goes over to him, makes up to him)* Pussycat, don't be like that with me. How can I help you?

GOEBBELS   My dear, Christine, I'm asking you, I'm begging you. I want you to tell me, in as few words as possible, what the Eleventh Olympic Games will do for the Third Reich.

CHRISTINE *(she again dries her hair, then stops)* Oh. That's easy, Joseph.

GOEBBELS   It is?

CHRISTINE   Yes, why on earth didn't you ask me before?

GOEBBELS   I'm asking you now.

CHRISTINE   Joseph, The Berlin Olympic Games will be the making of Germany.

Scene 5

Hitler's office. Hitler and Goebbels face each other, with Hitler holding a sheaf of papers. He throws them into a bin.

HITLER   Lewald's Report, Joseph. Absolute rubbish. Nothing more than a pottage of sentimental twaddle.

GOEBBELS   Exactly my opinion, Führer.

HITLER   All this Olympism stuff, all this garbage about goodwill and the brotherhood of man. Your Professor Lewald has quite lost contact with reality. This whole Olympic set-up, Joseph. It's absolutely crawling with Jews and Freemasons, you know that, don't you?

GOEBBELS   Common knowledge, Führer, common knowledge.

HITLER   And all that humbug about the glories of ancient Greece. Brutality and bum-boys, that was your Ancient Greece for you, Joseph. Sexual deviants, arse-bandits to a man, every single one of them.

GOEBBELS   No question of that, Führer. *(Pause)* But we are where we are. We are where we are.

HITLER *(exasperated)* And what exactly does that mean?

GOEBBELS   It means that either we cancel the Olympics now, or go full steam ahead. There really is no middle way.

HITLER   And which of these is it to be, in your considered opinion?

GOEBBELS *(decides to take the plunge)* Full steam ahead, Führer.

HITLER   Millions upon millions of Marks, Joseph. Enough to feed an army for ten years. Put your case.

GOEBBELS   The Olympics will be the making of Germany, Führer. They will provide us a unique showcase for the Reich, a once-in-a-lifetime chance to show the world that we, Germany, are the nation of the future. In August 1936, they will flock to the Fatherland in their thousands from the far ends of the earth. And we secure the theatre, the drama of sport, and all of its actors, four thousand of them, for virtually nothing, right here in Berlin, the heart of the Third Reich. We will enjoy a month, Führer, in which Germany will be at the absolute centre of the world's attention.

HITLER   Yes.

GOEBBELS   The civilised world will see our architecture, our sport, our art, our people.

HITLER   Everything that we want them to see...

GOEBBELS   Exactly. Worth a hundred ambassadors.

HITLER   A thousand, Joseph. A thousand.

GOEBBELS   Without a doubt.

HITLER   Joseph, none of what you are saying to me, none of it came from your Olympic fellow Professor Lewald, did it?

GOEBBELS *(po-faced)* No, not a single word of it, Führer. On my honour.

HITLER   I thought not. *(Pause)* But the Olympic Games — can we carry them off?

GOEBBELS   Undoubtedly, Führer. We have Speer – the man is a master at this sort of thing. And Carl Diem, our Olympic expert. The Third Reich is fully capable of producing the greatest Games of the modern era.

HITLER   Yes, we can. Of course we can. It will be just like another Nuremberg Rally.

GOEBBELS   And sport is the opium of the nation. Our people simply can't get enough of it, Führer. Our youth. The Games will give them a focus, an aim, a direction for all their energies.

HITLER   We will walk away with the moon.

GOEBBELS   Exactly, Führer.

HITLER   But medals, Joseph. These Olympics will be no good to us, to Germany, without medals.

GOEBBELS   No.

HITLER   So how many... how many Olympic medals?

GOEBBELS   Think of a number, Führer. Name a figure.

HITLER *(pause)* Thirty. Thirty gold medals.

GOEBBELS *(gulping)* Thirty GOLD medals? *(He gulps)* They will be yours, Führer. They will be yours. You have my word on it. *(He raises his arm in the "heil" salute.)*

Scene 6

SHIRER   20th September 1933 was the annual dinner of the Amateur Athletic Union, the governing body of American amateur sport and I was invited, as a guest. Avery Brundage, its chairman, got to his feet to give the annual address.

Tapping of spoon on glass to quieten the conversation of the diners.

BRUNDAGE   Ladies and Gentlemen, they say that the good Lord likes nothing better than a sinner come to repentance. Well I, Avery Brundage, am one such sinner. Let me take you back to 1912, to the Stockholm Olympic Games. I had gone there to compete in the pentathlon, but by the final event, the 1500 metres, I realised that I now had no chance of a medal, so what did I do? Ladies and gentlemen, I gave up, I chickened out, and that moment when I walked off the Stockholm track will remain with me for the rest of my born days. Like me, Major George Patton had travelled out to Sweden with high hopes of a medal in the modern pentathlon, an event specifically devised by Baron de Coubertin for military men. But Lady Luck had not smiled upon George in the very event where an army man might have expected to do well, the pistol competition. George has always claimed that one of his bullets had hit the bull through the same hole as his first shot, and that was why the officials couldn't find it, but those pesky Swedish judges did not agree! *(Laughter)* So he finished a long way down, and came into the final event, the cross-country well short of a medal. But that did not faze our George, not one little bit, Ladies and Gentlemen. No, George Patton had to be carried off on a stretcher after that cross-country — he fell flat on his face through the finishing tape — foaming at the mouth. But he ended up fifth, just short of a medal. So what is the moral of my little tale? It is that though the Lord loves winners, the Lord takes triers to his very bosom, and binds them firmly to him. And that is what the Olympic Games is all about, Ladies and Gentlemen, a man — or a woman — giving everything they have in mind and body. Now, some of you may well think it sacreligious that I take the name of the Lord to discuss sport. But to me, the Olympics, with its belief in ethics and fair play IS a religion. After all, where else will you find Christians, Muslims, Hindus and Jews all competing together in friendly rivalry? Only in the sacred field of sport, ladies and gentlemen, only in sport.

Enthusiastic applause.

Scene 7

Leni Riefenstahl's studio. Christine Muller, in fencing gear, holds a pose, as Leni, using a tripod, photographs her.

LENI　　　　OK.

CHRISTINE *(exhausted, drops her arm and shakes her head)* Have you got enough now?

LENI　　　　No, no. Just one more, I promise you. Then a break. From the front this time. Look straight at me.

CHRISTINE *(takes up a pose)* Like this?

LENI　　　　Yes, just like that, that's perfect — hold it there. Yes, look at me, stay still, hold it there. *(Pause)* Got it! *(Christine groans in relief, and puts her foil down)* Christine, you are a little star. Come here and let me hold you.

They embrace.

CHRISTINE   I thought you only liked muscular men, Miss Riefenstahl.

LENI   And muscular women, too, thank God. It gives me options.

They relax together.

CHRISTINE   He talks about you all the time, you know.

LENI   Goebbels? Nasty little man. Those groping hands...

CHRISTINE   Pussycat? He's OK. Joseph suits me, for the moment. You know where you are with him.

LENI   How's that?

CHRISTINE   Because Joseph will always let you down. *(Leni laughs)* Leni, he wants me to tell you something. The party want you to direct next year's Nuremberg Rally. Nearly half a million men, the biggest ever.

LENI   No. I made a film of the Rally this year, Christine. It was a total disaster. Organised chaos.

CHRISTINE   Joseph says next year will be different, Leni. Next year, the Rally will be drilled to perfection. Speer is involved now, and some army chaps, generals. It will be ballet in boots, I promise you.

LENI   No, never. Endless flags and soldiers marching up and down. A tyranny of tanks. It was awful. No, next year I want to go to Hollywood, like Dietrich.

CHRISTINE   Hollywood? Leni dear, you are incorrigible! The Rally is real, the Rally is the here and now. Nuremberg, it could be the very making of you, Leni. Might even get you the filming of the Olympics.

LENI   The Olympic Games?

CHRISTINE   Muscular men. Thousands of them. Man against man.

LENI   Man against himself. *(Pause)* The poetry of the body in action.

CHRISTINE   A mosaic of muscle. Day after hot, glorious summer day of it, Leni.

LENI   The 1936 Olympic Games. Now that, my dear Christine, is a horse of an entirely different colour.

Scene 8

SHIRER   Berlin, October 1933, in the partly-built 1916 Olympic Stadium, on a cold and windy autumn day. The foundations of the stadium can still just be seen through the weeds. Hitler is with Goebbels and Werner March, the son of the stadium's architect.

HITLER   Your father built well, March.

MARCH   He would have been proud to have been here with you today, Führer.

HITLER   And how many people would this 1916 stadium of his have held, had it been completed?

MARCH   Thirty thousand, Führer. I have my father's plans here.

HITLER   Joseph, make a note. One hundred thousand.

MARCH   One HUNDRED thousand? But... that will be impossible, Führer.

HITLER   Why?

MARCH   Over there. The Grunewald horse-racing track, Führer. It would have to be removed to make way for a stadium of such size.

HITLER   Then the track must be destroyed. *(Pause)* March, I want the 1936 stadium to be the greatest sports arena on the face of the earth, a worthy, a noble beginning of the thousand-year Reich. Can you deliver me such a stadium, March?

MARCH   Yes, Führer. I do believe that I can.

HITLER   Good, good. *(Pause)* And now, what about the Bell, March, now tell me all about the Bell!

MARCH *(flustered)* The Bell, Führer?

HITLER   We MUST have a Great Bell, March. It's common knowledge. Every stadium must have a Great Bell.

GOEBBELS *(sees his chance)* Of course. I have already designed the Great Bell, Führer. It will weigh precisely fifteen thousand kilos. Yes. The Great Olympic Bell. And we will build it here in Germany, in Bochum.

HITLER   Bochum. Excellent, excellent. And what about the inscription, Joseph? Every bell must have an inscription.

GOEBBELS   Simple, Führer. I can see your words now, carved around the rim of the Great Olympic Bell *(Pause)* "I CALL THE YOUTH OF THE WORLD".

HITLER   "I call the youth of the world." Perfect, Joseph. Perfect.

Scene 9

SHIRER   By November 1933, like many others, I became aware that Jews were being removed from every area of German public life. In the home of Theodore Lewald, he was again with his colleague, Carl Diem. But this time the conversation between the two men was of quite a different nature...

LEWALD   When did your letter arrive, Carl?

DIEM   The same day as yours, yesterday.

LEWALD   But Carl... but I can't get my head round any of this. I am not Jewish.

DIEM   Neither am I, Theodore. Just Liselott.

LEWALD   Your wife — Oh. I didn't know. *(Pause)* Me, it was my grandmother.

DIEM   That seems to be quite enough nowadays to lose a professorship.

LEWALD   It's all madness. Madness. They can't clear out the whole of Germany. Our doctors, our teachers, our judges? Half a million Jews?

DIEM   That is what it seems they are trying to do, Theodore. Someone from the Party told me yesterday that they were planning to send them all to Madagascar.

LEWALD   Madagascar? *(Pause)* Should we have seen this coming? The Jews are being banned from every sports club. Our colleagues at the International Olympic Committee, Carl, they won't stand for it, and as for us losing our professorships...!

DIEM   I wouldn't be too sure.

LEWALD   But they are cutting straight at the heart of Olympism, Carl, at everything we believe in, everything the Olympic Movement stands for. The Americans certainly won't tolerate it — they have lots of Jewish athletes.

DIEM   We'll see, Theodore, we'll see. Joseph Goebbels is no fool. He may have taken away our professorships but he's kept us on our Olympic committees.

LEWALD   Because they need us.

DIEM   But they don't WANT us. *(Pause)* What we must do now is to protect our families.

LEWALD   Yes. Yes. Our families.

DIEM   Say things we do not mean to people we do not like.

LEWALD   Worse still, say things we don't mean to people we DO like.

Scene 10

SHIRER   Everything happened so quickly, and me, I watched it happen — by April 1934 there was a Nazi boycott of Jewish shops, then Jews were forced out of all public positions, hell, they were even forbidden to employ German women below the age of forty. The cleansing of the race had begun almost immediately, a sort of crazy whirlwind of persecution, with no reason, no justice, no justification. There was simply no "why" in Germany any more. Then came the letter. It arrived with me right out of the blue, an invitation to the home of a certain Mr. and Mrs. Edwin Bergmann, of 21 Neustrasse, in Laupheim. It seemed to me they were being deliberately vague about the reason for the invitation, only that it somehow concerned the Berlin Olympics.

Shirer is with a middle-aged Jewish man Edwin Bergmann, who is dressed in a thick woollen cardigan. Edwin has two cups of tea, one of which he hands to Shirer.

EDWIN *(shouting)* Gretel, Gretel!

An athletic young woman appears with the homemade cakes — Gretel Bergmann.

GRETEL   Father.

EDWIN   This is Mr. Shirer, Gretel. Mr. Shirer is an American writer.

SHIRER   Nice to meet you, Gretel.

GRETEL   And you, sir.

EDWIN   My little Gretel here is an athlete, a high jumper. One metre fifty-two, Mr. Shirer.

SHIRER   Wow. That's over five feet.

EDWIN   Good stock, Mr Shirer. Good stock. I was a jumper myself, before the War. One metre seventy.

GRETEL   When there were no sandpits, Mr. Shirer, as Father never stops telling me.

EDWIN   Young people nowadays, Mr. Shirer. No respect anymore. No. An athlete must always come from good stock. We Jews have a saying — out of snow you can't make cheesecake.

SHIRER   So what do you want of me? How... how do you think can I be of help to you, Mr. Bergmann?

EDWIN   My brother in New York has told me about your articles in America, Mr. Shirer — reporting what is happening to Jews in Germany. Even in our sport.

SHIRER   But I have to weigh every word that I write, Mr. Bergmann, I have to be careful.

GRETEL   At my athletic club... no one there speaks to me, now. Even girls who used to be my best friends...

EDWIN   My daughter is treated like... like a leper. We are going to send Gretel over to friends in England, for safekeeping, Mr. Shirer, before things get any worse. But we still want her to compete for Germany in the Olympic Games... so... we would like you to record her progress in England, so that she cannot possibly be overlooked, when the team is finally chosen.

SHIRER   I get you. That's quite a story. So let's make a little deal, Gretel. You do the jumping, and I'll tell the world.

EDWIN   Thank you. An Olympic champion, even one of us, would be untouchable, Mr. Shirer.

Scene 11

SHIRER   Storm clouds were brewing for the Nazis, even the International Olympic Committee was beginning to express alarm at Hitler's treatment of the Jews. The IOC chairman Count Baillet-Latour took a personal interest and wrote to Avery Brundage and his colleague General Charles Sherrill in the States.

BAILLET-LATOUR *(French accent)* "I am not personally fond of Jews, or of Jewish influence. I know, for instance, that they frequently shout when they have no reason to do so but I will not have them molested in any way whatsoever. However, I have always been struck by the fact that the anti-semitic horrors that took place in Russia, the pogram never excited public opinion in the same way. Why? Because the Zionist propaganda was not made so cleverly."

SHERRILL   This letter from Latour, Avery — I'm not quite sure what he is trying to say...

BRUNDAGE   He's French.

SHERRILL   Belgian.

BRUNDAGE   Same thing.

SHERRILL   No question of it, this letter has got to come before our Olympic committee, and post-haste.

BRUNDAGE   I completely agree, Charles.

SHERRILL   Did you know those Nazis have built over fifty concentration camps?

BRUNDAGE   Concentration camps. And what exactly would they be?

SHERRILL   A bit like my boot camps, I would reckon. Gymnastics and long runs. Character-building stuff. But they've put Jews, communists and gypsies in these concentration camps, they're scooping whole families off the streets, hundreds of them.

BRUNDAGE   Reds and gypsies? All concentrated in one camp? Sounds to me as if those Nazis have got something good going for them there, Charles. We should take out a franchise.

SHERRILL   But that's not all, Avery. They've gone and banned Jews from all German sports clubs.

BRUNDAGE   Ah, sports clubs. Now that's an entirely different matter, Charles. They've crossed the line. That is directly contrary to Olympism and it's got to stop right now. Or else Uncle Sam is not taking a team to Berlin. We're not going. Not an American athlete will leave these shores.

Scene 12

SHIRER   The seeds of the American Olympic boycott movement had now been well and truly sown. Meanwhile, things were becoming difficult for Adolf Hitler — a weakening Deutschmark, possible trade embargos, even threats of mutiny in the SA, his military arm.

So the Chancellor did as he had always done in time of trial, he sought refuge in his mountain home, the Berghof.

Hitler sits at a table, reading. A servant enters.

SCHMIDT   Herr Goebbels is here, Führer.

HITLER   Thank you. The Strauss. Please select the Strauss. But don't play it yet.

Schmidt places a record ready to play on the gramophone. Goebbels enters and salutes.

GOEBBELS   Heil Hitler.

HITLER   I trust you had a good journey, Joseph?

GOEBBELS   Excellent, Führer. Excellent.

HITLER   I do hope you have some good news for me. This wretched Olympic fellow, Latour...

GOEBBELS   Not another letter?

HITLER   Yes. Always trying to grovel to those stinking American Jews and negroes. Latour is as slimy as a sack of snakes. The man should be a politician.

Schmidt enters.

SCHMIDT   Tea, Führer?

HITLER   Yes, thank you, Schmidt. Camomile. Settles the nerves. Joseph?

GOEBBELS   Coffee, black, for me.

HITLER   So what should we do about this wretched Belgian to keep him quiet about the Jews?

GOEBBELS   Latour? Simple, Führer. *(Pause for effect)* We give him Potemkin.

HITLER   Potemkin? Explain.

GOEBBELS   Count Potemkin, his derelict estates were due to be examined by Catherine the Great, so he simply put up fake buildings, mere pasteboard, with nothing behind them.

HITLER   As the Americans do in their western films.

GOEBBELS   You have it exactly, Führer. And in front of the pasteboard, Potemkin placed great crowds of smiling peasants to greet Catherine. And Catherine, she was delighted.

HITLER   Smiling Jews. Wonderful.

GOEBBELS   So we give our man Latour exactly what he wants to see. Potemkin.

HITLER   Everything he wants to see... but nothing. I like it. *(Pause)* I always look forward to your visits, Joseph. You never come to me with problems. Always solutions.

GOEBBELS   Thank you, Führer.

HITLER   Listen to this, Joseph, for just a moment. Just a snatch. *(He rises, places the needle on the record — Vienna Woods by Johanne Strauss)* Wonderful. Glorious.

GOEBBELS *(distant)* Indeed, Führer.

HITLER   You have no liking for Strauss?

GOEBBELS   No — Strauss. It... it's marvellous, marvellous.

HITLER   Strauss. That whole family. They sing with their hearts. German hearts. Blood and steel.

GOEBBELS   We have... I rather think we may have something of a problem there, Führer.

HITLER   A problem?

Schmidt enters with the tea.

SCHMIDT   Your tea, Führer.

HITLER   Turn that off, Schmidt. That'll be all for now.

Schmidt goes to the gramophone and the music stops. Exits.

HITLER   What problem?

GOEBBELS *(uneasily)* The blood, Führer. The blood. *(Pause)* You will know that we are checking back into the records... every one in public life...

HITLER   Of course. Essential. The blood. It's at the heart of everything we do. The cleansing of the German race.

GOEBBELS   Strauss. His great grandfather, Führer. *(Pause)* Jewish.

HITLER   Oh. Are you sure?

GOEBBELS   Yes, Führer. Absolutely certain.

HITLER   Mmm. His great grandfather. That must go back to 1800, Joseph. Perhaps even earlier.

GOEBBELS   Yes, Führer, earlier. 1786, to be exact.

HITLER   1786. Local records like that must be very difficult to locate.

GOEBBELS   Indeed they are, Führer.

HITLER   And equally easy to lose.

GOEBBELS   Indeed. Very easy to lose.

HITLER   And we must never, never for a single moment underestimate the incompetence of bureaucrats.

GOEBBELS   No, Führer. *(Pause)* Never. But... but what about the rules?

HITLER   The rules? Joseph, we ARE the rules.

Scene 13

The sound of girls chatting and laughing in the open air, the sound of "on your marks, get set," and a bang, a wooden high jump bar hitting the ground. It is training night at the London Polytechnic Athletic Club. Gretel approaches the Coach.

GRETEL   Excuse me, Frau... Miss.

COACH   Yes?

GRETEL   The lady over in the dressing room sent me here to the high jump.

COACH   Are you a club member?

GRETEL   No.

COACH   And what's your name?

GRETEL   Gretel... Gretel Bergmann, Miss.

COACH   Are you Swedish?

GRETEL   No, ma'am. German.

COACH   And you say you're a high jumper. *(She calls over to another athlete)* Put the bar down to three foot-six for Gretel, Mary.

GRETEL   How high is that, miss?

COACH   Three foot-six, Gretel... Oh. I see what you mean. About a metre, I suppose.

GRETEL   Could you put it up to one metre-fifty, Miss?

COACH   That's, that must be nearly five feet. That's a club record. Are you sure—?

GRETEL   Yes.

COACH   Are you all warmed up?

GRETEL   Yes.

COACH   One metre-fifty it is then. Put up the bar, please. On you go, Gretel.

A mime of high jump, followed by whoops and cheers.

COACH   Good grief! Well, it looks as if we've have found ourselves a jumper here, Ladies.

GRETEL   So am I allowed to join the club?

COACH   Of course. Why on earth not?

GRETEL   I'm Jewish.

COACH   And I'm Miss Goldstein. Welcome to the club.

Scene 14

SHIRER   In England that June of 1934, Gretel Bergmann cleared five feet, one inch to easily take the British title. She was now a potential Olympic medallist, and a member of the German national squad. Gretel had become a Potemkin Jew, sure and certain evidence of Nazi integrity. In that same summer Leni Riefenstahl prepared a script outline for *Triumph of the Will,* an account of the 1934 Nuremberg Rally. Hitler asked her to meet him in Berlin.

Hitler sits at his desk, with Leni Riefenstahl seated nervously in front of him.

HITLER   Would you like some camomile tea, Miss Riefenstahl? Always settles the nerves.

LENI   No thank you, Führer. *(Pause)* You... you have read my Nuremberg treatment?

HITLER   I did not realise that 'treatment' was the technical term, Miss Riefenstahl. Very interesting. *(Pause)* Yes, I have read your treatment, and your costings too. I must confess that until this moment I had no idea that the Third Reich could possess so many cameras.

LENI   A standard newsreel would require only a tenth of the cameras that I will employ in Nuremberg. But this will not be a mere newsreel, Führer, any more than a Rembrandt portrait is a photograph.

HITLER   Rembrandt.

LENI   Rembrandt. He touched the souls of those who sat for him.

HITLER   But Joseph — the Reichsminister says that you will film before and after the Rally, events that may not actually occur.

LENI   Yes. You see, this will be no mere record, Führer – it – it will be a... a vivid impression of a historic event. Every image on the screen will glorify you and the Reich. And it is in the juxtaposition of images, in the editing, that the effect is created.

It is not reality. It will be... something greater than reality, far beyond reality. A vision, a dream.

HITLER   My dream.

LENI   Yes, Führer. Your dream.

HITLER   And it must be about the German people, Miss Riefenstahl. Our might... And our right. Your film must lift the hearts of the nation.

LENI   It will, I promise you. It will show us as we are, Führer. And as we would wish to be.

HITLER   As we would wish to be. Yes.

LENI   And I have already had an idea, Führer, on how you will appear, on your first arrival in Nuremberg.

HITLER   Yes?

LENI   You will come soaring into Nuremberg from the sky, out of the clouds, like... like Zeus.

HITLER   Yes. Like Zeus. *(Pause)* Like Zeus. Like a God.

Scene 15

We see the Ohio State coach Larry Snyder standing, holding aloft a starting pistol.

SNYDER   On your marks. *(Pause)* Get set. *(Pause)*

The gun cracks, and there is the scratch of spikes, Jesse seen in slow motion running. The cheers of athletes, "great run, Jesse, etc". Jesse Owens, in running kit, breathing heavily and sweating, joins Coach.

JESSE   How'd I do, Coach?

SNYDER   Five point nine seconds for sixty yards, Jesse.

JESSE   Five nine! That's the best I've ever run, Coach.

SNYDER   It was garbage, Jesse. Garbage. You stood up out of your holes. You gotta stay DOWN ! I must have told you that a hundred times.

A track-suited athlete appears.

ATHLETE *(timidly)* Coach Snyder...

SNYDER   Can't you see I'm talking to Jesse here?

ATHLETE   It... it's a Mr. Shirer to see you, sir.

SNYDER   Then why didn't you speak up and say so? Welcome to Ohio State University, Mr. Shirer.

SHIRER   Thank you, Coach.

SNYDER   And this is my boy, Jesse.

SHIRER   Nice to meet you, Jesse.

JESSE   And you, sir.

SNYDER   I'll leave you two here to chew the fat, Mr. Shirer — I got me some fool high jumpers down there who can't seem to get their dumb asses off the deck. See you later. *(Leaves)*

SHIRER   Coach Snyder has told you all about me?

JESSE   That you weren't a sports writer?

SHIRER   Yes. I wanted to write about some of the things that don't always make it to the sports pages, Jesse.

JESSE   Not much to tell, Mr. Shirer.

SHIRER   OK. So let's start off with your parents, your father.

JESSE   My father, he was a sharecropper, dirt-poor. He came up to Cleveland from Alabama, looking for work.

SHIRER   Must have been a hard life for you. Brothers or sisters?

JESSE   Nine, sir, so a boy had to be real quick to get to his chitlings.

SHIRER   And when — how old were you when you found out that you were fast?

JESSE   I would reckon about twelve, at Fairview High, it was my coach, Mr. Riley. Coach Riley, he was a good man, he trained me in the morning before school, because I had to work evenings in a shoe shop, to pull in a few bucks.

SHIRER   And I hear tell that you are married now?

JESSE   Two months back. We have one child, Gloria. She's three.

SHIRER   No need for you to work in a shoe shop now, Jesse.

JESSE   No sir, now I pump gas.

SHIRER   But you have a sports scholarship, to pay your way through college?

JESSE   No sir, no way. No nigra boy here at Ohio State has a scholarship, Mr. Shirer. That's for white boys. My wife Ruth, she takes in white folks' laundry, and serves table here, and me, Coach Snyder got me the job at the gas station. That's how I get to pay for college.

SHIRER   No scholarship? But Jesse, you — you have to be one of the greatest athletes on earth.

JESSE   But I'm black, Mr. Shirer. Black.

SHIRER   OK, OK, Jesse, so let me start by asking you this — how much do you know about the move back East to boycott the Berlin Olympics?

JESSE *(disturbed)* Boycott? What boycott?

SHIRER   Ours, America's. The Olympic Boycott Movement, it's building up a big head of steam back in New York.

JESSE   Let me get this clear, Mr. Shirer. You're telling me that America might not go to Berlin?

SHIRER   Yes. It's possible.

JESSE   This is bad, Mr. Shirer. I don't know much about politics, but there must be some way to fix this.

SHIRER   It's because of the Jews, Jesse. Jewish athletes. Hitler, the Nazis, won't let them compete in German sports.

JESSE   So, what have those Jews done?

SHIRER   They haven't done anything at all, Jesse. It's just because the Nazis hate the Jews.

JESSE   So I... we don't get to go to the Olympics, just because of the Jews?

SHIRER   Yes.

Snyder appears.

SNYDER   Sorry to interrupt you, Mr. Shirer. Jesse and I got a lot more work to do. Don't want my boy here to cool off.

SHIRER   Thanks, Coach. I think I've got just about all I need now.

SNYDER   Broad jump, Jesse. Get you down there and measure up your approach run. And just remember you got a following wind up your ass.

JESSE *(distant, still troubled)* Yes, Coach. I got you.

SHIRER   So long, Jesse. And the very best of luck next week in the Nationals. Make sure you bring back gold to Ohio Campus.

SNYDER *(interrupting, sharp)* No nigra allowed to live on Ohio State Campus, Mr. Shirer. Never has been, never will be, leastways, not while I am around.

Scene 16

SHIRER   Day by day, week by week, things were getting worse for German Jews, who were now arriving on the east coast of America in increasing numbers, and the Olympic boycott movement gradually gained momentum. So, in the autumn of 1934, Avery Brundage travelled to Paris to meet with the IOC president, Count Baillet-Latour.

SFX Soft sounds of exclusive men's club. The clink of glasses.

BRUNDAGE   Santé, Count.

LATOUR   Santé. Please feel free to call me Henri, Avery.

BRUNDAGE   Thank you, Henri.

LATOUR   You will, of course, understand that as vice-president of the IOC, I must above all protect the Olympic Games, the Olympic Movement, its ideals and its future, its legacy, so to speak.

BRUNDAGE   That goes without saying, Henri.

LATOUR   And it is my feeling — and let me assure you that I have nothing against them — that the Jews, though intelligent, can often be unscrupulous. Many of my friends are Jews, but, you know Avery, the Jews are a race who must always be kept within... certain limits.

BRUNDAGE   Naturally.

LATOUR   But, and here I must be frank, I must tell you that there is a strong and growing feeling here in Europe that the American move to boycott the Olympic Games is almost certainly nothing less than a cunning Zionist plot.

BRUNDAGE   A Zionist plot! You have some direct proof of this?

LATOUR   Yes. But it is obvious. The proof is everywhere you look, Avery, staring us straight in the face. Let me ask you a question, Avery. Correct me if I am in error. I believe that the best basketball players in America are Jews.

BRUNDAGE   You are well-informed, Henri. They are indeed.

LATOUR   But do you know the reason, Avery? Because basketball is a sport which requires cunning, and your Jew is cunning as a fox. And this Zionist plot to undermine the Olympic Games is merely an excellent example of that cunning.

BRUNDAGE   Zionists. You will have to give me some hard proof to take back with me, Henri.

LATOUR   I have it, Avery, all the necessary evidence. Here is a file, from the German government. One hundred and five pages. *(Hands over a bulky file)*

BRUNDAGE   Thank you. This will take a lot of reading.

LATOUR   Let me be absolutely clear, Avery. For the IOC, an

Olympics without the United States of America – that would be quite unthinkable.

BRUNDAGE   Indeed Henri, for me Olympism and its ideals has always been a way of life.

LATOUR   As it has been for me, Avery. *(Pause)* Which leads me to this. There just might soon be a vacancy for another IOC member... someone of quality who might take my place as chairman. *(Pause)* In due course.

BRUNDAGE   But surely... surely America already has its full complement of members, Henri?

LATOUR   Yes and no. I have no mandate to explain more to you at this point.

BRUNDAGE   Chairman designate.

LATOUR   Yes. You might choose to call it that.

BRUNDAGE   That would be a great honour, Henri.

LATOUR   But a much-deserved one, Avery, much-deserved *(Pause)*. So you see that it is absolutely essential that this information on the Zionists reach your American colleagues. *(Pause)* And that they reach the appropriate conclusion.

BRUNDAGE   I'll make sure of that, Henri.

Scene 17

SHIRER   By early 1935, Leni Riefenstahl was able to show her Führer the final cut of *Triumph of the Will*, and Hitler was delighted with it; a masterpiece of propaganda. The contract to direct the film of the 1936 Olympic Games was a formality, and Leni's preparations began.

Leni and Christine are in Leni's study. Leni is setting out her storyboard for the Olympic film — or drying off negatives/prints, etc. Christine is assisting. Windt's stirring music from the stadium sequence.

LENI   Windt sent me this section of his score. He hasn't quite finished it yet, but he let me have it. It's for the opening sequence. Sets the tone of the film. What do you think?

CHRISTINE   Sounds marvellous, Leni. Like *Ben Hur*. Epic.

LENI   The Olympic Games IS epic. Giving everything you have in competition is always epic. You're an athlete, you should know that better than me.

CHRISTINE   So how will you start your film?

LENI   Back — I'll start way back, in the ruins of Olympia, with my camera gliding like a ghost through the ruined temples. Then, then, a sort of ballet of athletes, naked men running and jumping and throwing, just like the Ancient Games.

CHRISTINE   Mmm. Naked? You might just get off with that. Art.

LENI   Yes, and Carl Diem has created this marvellous torch relay through Europe, to Berlin, after the vestal virgins light the sacred flame at Olympia.

CHRISTINE   Vestal virgins? They might be rather hard to find.

LENI   So I will have this relay of naked runners carry the torch all the way across Greece...

CHRISTINE   Hold it there, Leni. Naked men, running all the way across Greece? First the American censors will cut your film to ribbons. You've seen American movies, Leni — they're fully-clothed even when they are making love, AND they make the actors keep one foot on the floor.

LENI   And second?

CHRISTINE   Simple anatomy, darling. Women wobble on top, men wobble down below.

LENI   Mmm, you've got a point there, Christine. The runners' feet would be torn to shreds.

CHRISTINE   Yes. Don't forget their poor feet, darling.

LENI   So it's sandals and shorts for the relay. Very short.

CHRISTINE *(quietly)* Leni — a word to the wise — Joseph doesn't like you. You've got much too close to his beloved Führer. Are you really going to be happy working for him?

LENI   I rather think I can cope with your pussycat, Christine.

CHRISTINE   And what about the Party? Are you sure you've got the stomach to work with thugs like Goering and Himmler?

LENI   The Nazis? Don't forget I did it in Nuremberg. And remember, my dear Christine, if Michelangelo had agonised about the morals of the Medicis, then we would not now enjoy the glories of the Sistine Chapel.

Scene 18

SHIRER   Meanwhile, over in New York, there was one American who was now standing up for the Jews, a man coming from left field, none other than an Irish-American, Judge Jeremiah Mahoney, who had just taken over from Avery Brundage as head of the Amateur Athletic Union, representing the governing bodies of every American sport.

Sounds of restaurant. A waiter puts a cloth on the table and sets the chairs.

SHIRER   So there was I, on one of my first big assignments pencil poised, having lunch with the Judge in February of 1935, at New York Athletic Club.

Mahoney comes in during this, his hat and coat are taken by the waiter. He looks round for Shirer.

MAHONEY   Shirer? *(They shake hands.)* So exactly where is this Olympic article of yours going to appear, Mr. Shirer?

SHIRER   The *Washington Post*. And it will be syndicated, sir, throughout the country.

MAHONEY   Good. Then let's get down to business right away, young man. You know all about me. Started with nothing but a hole in my sock, when the only way an Irish boy like me could make it out of the tenements was with his bare mitts.

SHIRER   It wasn't easy being Irish in your day, sir?

MAHONEY   It still isn't, not even now. Not much different from the Jews—

WAITER   Your table's ready, sir.

MAHONEY   —but I can't complain, Shirer. America has been good to me.

SHIRER   Your Olympic boycott group, sir...

MAHONEY   Yes. I suppose you've heard that my good friend Avery Brundage has been putting it around that I am being bank-rolled by Jewish businessmen, Zionists?

SHIRER   No, sir. I thought he was all for the boycott?

MAHONEY   Not now. Avery's a self-made man, Shirer, always had his eye for the main chance. Lost his shirt in '29, then pulled himself up by his bootstraps. Chicago, in the construction business. Full of crooks. Brundage is a millionaire twice over.

SHIRER   So what exactly does he get out of it?

MAHONEY   He's looking for status, and plenty of it. Sport is like Mom and apple pie, Shirer. Everybody loves it. And the Olympics, that's the big bazonka. You get to hang out with presidents and kings, and once every four years you get to run the best muscle in the world. Even President Franklin Delano Roosevelt himself doesn't get to do that.

Waiter enters with two whiskeys.

WAITER   Compliments of the house, Gentlemen.

SHIRER   But surely Brundage is on public record against going to Berlin, I read it back in 1933.

MAHONEY   You're right, Shirer. But that was 1933. Someone big over in Europe has got to Brundage, I'd put my last dollar on it. Tempted him. They're lining Brundage up for something special, an American IOC place, though I don't know how, 'cos we've got our full Olympic allotment already. It's as plain as the nose on your face. Top table for Avery Brundage from now on. At last he's in the International Big League.

SHIRER   So he's willing to give the German Jews the bum's rush?

MAHONEY   Got it in one, my boyo. You see, we've got plenty of millionaires in the world, Shirer, but only one Olympic Games – the greatest show on earth.

SHIRER   What do you propose to do, sir?

MAHONEY   Fight Brundage every inch of the way, that's what. Those Nazis are just gangsters in jackboots, Shirer. They make Al Capone look like one of the Dead End Kids. If we go to Berlin next year, it'll be like handing the Nazis a blank cheque. But I've got me an ace in the hole, Shirer. You see, it doesn't matter a rat's patootie if Brundage and our Olympic committee decides to send a team to Berlin. No, it's my people, the Amateur Athletic Union, WE own the athletes. We're the men who run American sports, so we own the athletes. So I'll work my butt off getting out the vote for a boycott at the AAU Conference in December. In the meantime, I'm sending our top man, General Charles Sherrill, over to Germany on a fact-finding mission, to get at the truth. Our Charles will sort those Nazis out, you mark my words, Shirer. Just you mark my words.

Scene 19

Hitler and Goebbels are listening to a choir sing the Olympic Hymn at a concert.

HITLER   General Sherrill, Joseph. Your dossier on him. Excellent work.

GOEBBELS   Thank you, Führer.

HITLER   That English writer, John Buchan. He has a phrase... let me try to bring it to mind... I have it... The tiger's picture is outside, a man's picture is inside.

GOEBBELS   I will remember that, Führer.

HITLER   Your report, Joseph, that is the outside picture, but it nevertheless contains vital clues. About the character, the nature of this fellow General Charles Sherrill. The inside picture.

GOEBBELS   Yes, Führer?

HITLER   Our American general admires Mussolini and Ataturk.

GOEBBELS   Yes?

HITLER   So our General Sherrill likes order, Joseph.

GOEBBELS   Order and discipline. Yes.

HITLER   And that is exactly what we will deliver to him, when he arrives in Germany. Order and discipline. Row upon row of it.

Scene 20

Sounds of construction, tractors etc.

SHIRER   The construction of the 1936 Olympic stadium was underway, with no expense spared. One day in the spring of 1935, Leni and Christine stood in the earthworks as the great stadium slowly took shape around them.

Leni has a camera and is working out what she intends to do. Christine helps with gear and sketches of the groundplans. She is cold and fed up.

LENI   Can you see it, Christine, can you see it?

CHRISTINE   Sorry, Leni. Only men and mud. Only men and mud.

LENI   I can see it all, I can see everything. Down there, I'll have a camera on rails, so that I can follow the runners all the way up the finishing straight.

CHRISTINE   All I can see is a couple of tractors.

LENI   And up there...

CHRISTINE   Where?

LENI   There, up there, in the sky... I'll have a camera in a balloon, running all day, directly above the track.

CHRISTINE   But how on earth do you control the camera?

LENI   You can't. You just have to let it run all day.

And hope that you might get something.

CHRISTINE   So how many metres of film will you use?

LENI   Maybe a million metres. I don't care.

CHRISTINE   A million metres! That's half way round the world.

LENI   I'll edit it, Christine.

CHRISTINE   You can see it all, can't you?

LENI   No, I can't. That's what makes sport so wonderful — all these great athletes coming here to us, here in Berlin, from the four corners of the earth. Who wins, who loses, nobody knows for certain.

CHRISTINE   Only one certain winner, Leni.

LENI   Who?

CHRISTINE   Hitler.

Scene 21

Judge Mahoney's office. Mahoney stands reading a newspaper. There is a door knock.

MAHONEY   Come in. *(Jesse Owens enters)* Jesse, my boy!

JESSE   Sir.

MAHONEY   Sit you down right there, Jesse, my boy. *(Looks at the newspaper and shakes his head)* Six world records in forty-five minutes. Amazing. Absolutely amazing. As of now, you are the greatest athlete on the planet, Jesse. Every black athlete in America looks up to you.

JESSE   Thank you, Judge.

MAHONEY   Let me say right away that nothing we discuss here will leave this room. Not a word. Everything will be strictly between the two of us, man to man.

JESSE   That's fine by me, sir.

MAHONEY   First of all, my apologies we couldn't keep our date at the New York Athletics Club. Wasn't a table to be had in the whole house.

JESSE   No problem, Judge. The club got many black members?

Mahoney does not answer.

MAHONEY   Let me get right to the point, Jesse. I need your help.

JESSE   Anything I can do. Just ask.

MAHONEY   It's really quite simple, Jesse. Go out and talk to your people. Get your boys to pull out of the Olympic Games.

JESSE   My boys?

MAHONEY   Black athletes. They all look up to you.

JESSE   No, Judge, I can't do that.

MAHONEY   Why not?

JESSE   First, because no man on earth can tell those "boys" what to do. They would just laugh straight in my face.

MAHONEY   And second?

JESSE   Let me try to lay it right on the line with you, Judge. *(Pause)* You know we have some great black ball-players.

MAHONEY   Of course.

JESSE   But just how many blacks do we have in pro baseball and pro football teams? How many? Not one.

MAHONEY   Nothing much I can do about that, Jesse.

JESSE   That's not the way we hear it, Judge. Your AAU people – they run American sports, they decide who plays and who doesn't. They could change everything for us blacks tomorrow, if they had a mind to.

MAHONEY   I think we'll have to let that fly stick to the wall, Jesse.

JESSE   That's one lallapaloosa of a fly, Judge.

MAHONEY   OK, OK, so let's say you have a point there, Jesse, and what say I bring it up with my committee in January, after our Olympic vote. Maybe then we can rustle up something. Get a better deal for your people. So just you leave it with me. But surely, don't you realise what Hitler thinks of Negro athletes, Jesse?

JESSE   Yes. He calls us America's Black Auxiliaries. Had to look it up in the dictionary. But that Herr Hitler, he got it right. WE ARE auxiliaries.

MAHONEY   But you are part of the American team, Jesse.

JESSE   No, Judge, we have two teams. You really think I'll be rooming up with some white guy on that boat to Berlin? And any black boy as much as looks at a white girl on that crossing, he won't put on a spike in the Olympic Games, take my word for that, Judge.

MAHONEY   But, come on Jesse. What about the German Jews? Don't you give a damn for what is happening to those people? Nothing at all?

JESSE   Those Jews, they're getting a raw deal, judge, no question of that, but we blacks, we've been getting pretty much the same deal here for hundreds of years. My grandfather was a slave, Judge – a slave. But black athletes pulling out of Berlin? None of my people think it will change a thing for those German Jews.

MAHONEY   So... you're telling me, the Chairman of your National Association that you can't — you won't — get behind me on this?

JESSE   Let me be straight with you, Judge. If your people in the AAU, if they take a vote in December and they tell us we don't go to Berlin, then that's it, we won't go. But you won't get black athletes to boycott the Olympics, and that's a fact.

MAHONEY   So — let me get this clear — you are telling me for absolute certain that you won't speak out for a boycott of the

Berlin Olympic Games?

JESSE   Judge, track and field, running and jumping, that's pretty much the only sport in America where we blacks can compete on the same field as whites. If I can come back from Berlin with some gold medals, then I might get me an agent who can find me some paid work, make a few bucks.

MAHONEY   But come on, Jesse, what kind of work might that be? We've got no professional track and field now in America, it's not like baseball. You wouldn't make a dime here after Berlin, Jesse. Not a dime. Get real, son.

JESSE   Vaudeville, novelty races, maybe even a black movie. Not much, not the front of the Wheaties box like if I were white, but enough to put down a few bucks on a house, maybe buy Minnie and me a little laundry. Something like that, something I would never get, if I weren't fast. *(Pause)* Judge, let me say it like it is. My legs are all I've got. *(Pause)*

MAHONEY   Jesse, has a gentleman by the name of Avery Brundage been in touch with you?

JESSE   Last week. He seems to be a very fine man.

MAHONEY   So they say.

JESSE   And Mr. Brundage, he said something to me that made me stop and think.

MAHONEY   And exactly what would that be?

JESSE   Two of our Jewish hundred metre men, fast boys, George Stolle and Marty Glickman, they say that they are going to be on that boat to Berlin, Judge. Your Herr Hitler and his Nazis don't seem to bother them much.

Scene 22

General Sherrill's Press Conference.

CHAIRMAN   General Sherrill will now answer your questions, Ladies and Gentlemen, on the results of his fact-finding visit to Germany.

POWELL   Powell, *New York Times*, General. Is it true that you were a dash man way back, and that you invented the crouch start?

SHERRILL   Yes and no, young man. I WAS a dash man — a hundred yards, that was my best distance — but no, I didn't actually invent the crouch start, that was my coach, the late Mike Murphy. But I was the first man to use it in competition. Caused quite a stir at the time, as I remember it.

SMITH   Smith, *Chicago Herald*. You are causing quite a stir NOW, General. They say that since coming back from Germany you have given those Nazis a clean bill of health.

SHERRILL   Not at all, Mr. Smith, not at all. But may I remind you that my task was not to judge the German political system, it was to give the German sports programme a thorough investigation. And, let me tell you, it was magnificent, an example to us all. [The Germans are a great sporting nation.]

SMITH   But what about the Jews, General?

SHERRILL   I spent four whole days at Herr Hitler's home, the Berghof, as his honoured guest. And the Chancellor solemnly assured me that no German Jew who had reached the required standard would be denied entry to the Olympic Games.

SMITH   Do you have any names you can give us?

SHERRILL   Of Jewish athletes? There's young Gretel Bergmann, the high jumper. She's just won the British title. And Helen Mayer, the fencer — she's in California, but she's going back to Germany for their trials.

POWELL   So why exactly do you think so many of our unions and our Jewish groups are still opposed to us going to Berlin, General?

SHERRILL   Communists, Mr Powell, every man jack of them, Reds to a man. [Hitler has cleared commie scum like these out of Germany, and if we had any sense we would be doing exactly the same here in the United States of America.]

MARLOW   Marlow, *Seattle News*. What was your personal impression of Herr Hitler, General?

SHERRILL   Herr Hitler's face and figure showed he is in perfect health — good colour, but not too much, well-built, but not too heavy, good height but not really tall. His eye is clear, his glance is frank, his replies prompt but limited. There was no speechifying, such as our politicians are liable to use, even to an audience of one.

MARLOW   So is Herr Hitler a man you think we Americans can do business with?

SHERRILL   Unquestionably, Miss Marlow. Never until I met him did I understand how he gathered the personal following that started his Nazi movement, but now I do.

SHIRER   Shirer, *Washington Post*. General, with your permission, I would like to read you a short quotation from a recent sports book, written by a German officer, a Major Bruno Malitz, and given the formal approval of the German government.

SHERRILL   Feel free, Mr. Shirer. Feel free.

SHIRER   Here it is, and let me be clear — what I have here is a direct quotation, General. "Jewish sports leaders, like the Jewish plague, have absolutely no place in German sport. They are worse than the rampaging hordes of Barbarians, famine, floods, drought, locusts and poison gas — the Jews are far worse than all these horrors."

SHERRILL   That statement, Mr. Shirer, is a vile fiction. A vile fiction.

SHIRER   It comes straight from Berlin, General, so it is an official document. And there is plenty more, all pretty much in the same vein. And I have here a copy of the original, in German, if you wish to examine it, sir.

Tumult and gavel banging.

CHAIRMAN   That concludes today's conference, Gentlemen.

Scene 23

SHIRER   So it was clear to me that the temperature in the USA was rising, and rising fast, and it was a decidedly nervous Avery Brundage who decided to put in a call to Count Henri Baillet-Latour.

BRUNDAGE   Is that you, Henri?

LATOUR   Yes, Avery, and you are coming through very clearly.

BRUNDAGE   We may have ourselves a little problem here in America. You know that the AAU vote on an Olympic boycott is coming up soon?

LATOUR   December sixth, is that correct?

BRUNDAGE   Yes. And I need to have me a fall-back position, Henri.

LATOUR   Fall-back? I do not quite understand.

BRUNDAGE   A fall-back. *(Pause)* Somewhere to go, an alternative plan of action, in the event of a "no" vote.

LATOUR   But... but... Avery, a "no" vote? That is surely quite inconceivable.

BRUNDAGE   But not impossible, Henri. Not impossible. So I — we have to make plans... to deal with that eventuality.

LATOUR   So what exactly do you propose?

BRUNDAGE   That in the event of a "no" vote, that we ignore that vote, and my Olympic Committee will send its own American Olympic team to Berlin.

(Pause)

LATOUR   That... that sounds very strange. In America, who controls your athletes?

BRUNDAGE   The AAU — but as far as selection for the Olympic Games is concerned, we do. Our Olympic Association. I DO.

LATOUR   But if your American athletes defy their AAU, their national governing body, and come to Berlin, won't they be punished in some way?

BRUNDAGE   Possibly, but they will all have to take that chance, Henri. That will be entirely up to them.

LATOUR   But Avery, do you believe that in such a case you could deliver me a fully representative American team?

BRUNDAGE   They, every athlete in America, will all want to be on that boat to Berlin, guarantee it, Henri. So my team — the American team — will be entirely representative, I assure you. The cream of the crop. The greatest athletes on earth in Berlin.

LATOUR   Then I can see no possible grounds for any objection, Avery. After all, our relationship has never been at any time with the AAU, but always with you and your National Olympic Committee. But, my dear Avery, let this be your fall-back position only. *(Pause)* And please inform no one else, I beg of you. Keep this between the two of us.

BRUNDAGE   You have my word on that, Henri.

Scene 24

SHIRER   It is now November, 1935. There are only just over two months to the opening of the Winter Olympics at Garmisch Partenkirchen and only a month to the vital AAU vote on an Olympic boycott.

Hitler and Goebbels are, standing at an open window, silent. Then we hear the clanging of the Great Olympic Bell. The two men hear it sound four times. Hitler nods.

HITLER   Magnificent.

GOEBBELS   Perfect pitch.

HITLER *(nods)* Thank you. You can close the window now, Joseph. *(Goebbels closes the window)* December 6th. The American vote. Where are we now?

GOEBBELS   We must see what transpires, Führer.

HITLER   Transpires? I thought that the vote was all arranged.

GOEBBELS   It is not really possible to... arrange Americans, Führer.

HITLER   But haven't we bought this fellow Brundage?

GOEBBELS   Not exactly. Men like Brundage are difficult to buy, Führer.

HITLER   Difficult to buy? You told me he had worked in Chicago.

GOEBBELS   Brundage has promised us his complete support.

HITLER   But is it certain the vote will go in our favour?

GOEBBELS   Nothing is absolutely certain, Führer.

HITLER   Joseph, I have put 33 million Reichmarks into your Olympics, nearly three times more than the Americans in Los Angeles. We have hundreds of athletes in full-time training, and we have fifty million Germans who expect us to deliver the greatest Games of the modern era. If the Americans don't vote to come, it will domino, and the English and their Empire will follow. We will be finished, you understand that, don't you? *(Goebbels is silent.)* And don't ever forget, Joseph, they are all out there in the darkness, just waiting for me to fail.

GOEBBELS   Who, Führer?

HITLER   Those scum who have hated me from the start — our generals, von this and von that. They all want the corporal to fail, every one of them...

GOEBBELS   The American vote will go with us, Führer. Brundage has assured me that he has the necessary votes. You have the word of Joseph Goebbels on it.

HITLER   Your word? Good. Good. We have come much too far to fail now. *(Pause)* Now, are there any other issues?

Goebbels takes a file from the table, withdraws a letter from it and nervously examines it.

GOEBBELS   Only one matter of any real importance, Führer. Our ice hockey team, for the Winter Olympics.

HITLER   Yes?

GOEBBELS   One of our top players, Rudi Ball, is a Jew.

HITLER   Then Ball cannot possibly play. Where is the problem?

Goebbels hands Hitler the letter from the file.

GOEBBELS   From our leading player, Gustav Jaenecke.

Hitler scrutinises the letter, then lays it on the table.

HITLER   Jaenecke says he will not play for us in the Olympics.

GOEBBELS   No, Führer. Not without Rudi Ball.

HITLER   Does he have the slightest idea of the consequences?

GOEBBELS   Yes, Führer, I really think he does. But if he refuses to play in the Olympics, it will be a slap in the face for us, for Germany, no matter what we do to him later. And people will say — if we cannot control our athletes, how can we possibly control Germany?

HITLER   Just how good a player is this man, Jaenecke?

GOEBBELS   He is our best player, Führer.

Hitler picks up the letter, stands, goes behind his chair and, hands behind his back, paces up and down as Goebbels nervously waits for his decision.

GOEBBELS   So?

Hitler suddenly turns, tears the letter to pieces and hurls it to the floor.

HITLER *(spitting it out)* The Jew plays, Joseph. The Jew plays.

Scene 25

The AAU Annual General Meeting. December 6th. General hubbub.

CHAIRMAN Gentlemen, Gentlemen, order please. *(Silence)* Mr. Brundage has the floor.

BRUNDAGE Thank you, Mr. Chairman. I have here in my hands a dozen editorials from Negro newspapers and journals, Ladies and Gentlemen, every single one of them supporting American attendance at the Berlin Olympics. And I have here an equal number of letters from Jewish athletes, begging me to put their case for Uncle Sam's going to Berlin. My appeal to each one of you is — don't let our athletes down!

MAHONEY Mr. Brundage, I have spoken to our Negro and our Jewish athletes — and you are right — most of them want to go, but all of them have said to me that they want us, their leaders to make that decision for them. We are the guardians of American sport, and they will abide by whatever we decide.

BRUNDAGE And it is our responsibility to sport, our responsibility to the Olympic movement to keep the Olympic flame alive, Mr. Mahoney.

MAHONEY Not at the expense of the very standards, the beliefs which it was created to uphold!

BRUNDAGE The German authorities have given us an express commitment that no German Jew who has reached the required standard will be omitted.

MAHONEY And how, how in God's name are they to do that when they are denied training facilities and coaching?

BRUNDAGE Three German Jews are in their Olympic squad, Rudi Ball, Helen Meyer and Gretel Bergmann.

MAHONEY Meyer lives in California and Bergmann in England!

BRUNDAGE Gentlemen, our European friends are closer to the German situation than we are, and not a single European nation — except Communist Spain — has so far withdrawn from the Olympics. And the English athletes have voted by a hundred votes to three to go to Berlin. Isn't that enough?

MAHONEY Gentlemen of the AAU, [if we go to Berlin we

endorse the Nazi thugs and everything they stand for. But] if we pull out now, America sends out a message loud and clear to the civilised world. Over there in Europe they're all sitting there, just waiting for Uncle Sam to show the way. If we stay out, I'll bet a dollar to a dime that the Brits and the French will do the same, and Herr Hitler's Nazi Olympics will go straight down the tubes. And no Olympics means no Master Race.

BRUNDAGE   Mr. Chairman, I really must protest. What we are getting here is politics, not sport. It is not the role of the AAU to engage in the political arena. The Olympic Games are far above politics.

MAHONEY   Mr. Chairman, it is not we in the AAU who have brought politics into sport, but Hitler and his fascist gang — by their persecution of our Jewish brothers! Let me ask you this. Who was it who said, in 1933, and I quote directly, 'It will be absolutely impossible for the United States to take a team to Germany if the Nazis did not subscribe to Olympic ideals?' I'll tell you who — none other than the gentleman standing here at my side — Mr. Avery Brundage !

BRUNDAGE   A blatant lie! Taken out of context!

MAHONEY   But let me end by putting the case to you in very personal terms. I want each man here to be able to look himself in the mirror tomorrow and say — yes, I stood up for those Jewish athletes who were forced to train on farmer's fields — yes, I stood up for all those Jewish coaches and officials who were kicked out of their clubs — yes, I stood up for the beliefs that run through Olympic sport like blood through an athlete's body — the right to train and compete regardless of race, creed or colour. And yes, I stood up for the ideals that have made the United States of America the greatest nation on earth!

CHAIRMAN   Gentlemen, I think that we have now given this topic a full and thorough debate. We will now take a vote.

Scene 26

Hubbub, then the ringing of a bell, the noise of the AAU committee dropping to silence.

CHAIRMAN   Gentlemen, we now have the result of the ballot. Against attending the 1936 Berlin Olympic Games — 48.5 votes. For attendance — 51 votes. The United States will therefore compete in the 1936 Berlin Olympic Games!

Scene 27

The stadium, 1948, action as at beginning of the play, sound of planes overhead, spotlight on Shirer.

SHIRER   When I stand out here in the stadium, and look around me and see what we are doing now to help these Berliners, the sky black with planes, and I look back on 1936, I think why did we do nothing? Could I have done more? Of course, I wrote thousands of words, that was what I was paid to do, and I spoke to athletes, dozens of them. But that guy, that athlete, he lived only for that moment, that moment when he could run, jump and throw at the Olympic Games, that was all that mattered to him, not some far-off German Jew.

And so we all went to Berlin, and it was marvellous, the greatest Olympic Games in history. Marvellous and terrible, all at the same time, and I knew it, I knew it when I saw Jesse Owens fly up the track, and years later when Leni Riefenstahl's film made those athletes into Gods. And ten years later, so many of those young men lie in cold, unmarked graves all over Europe.

And — before I forget — do you remember little Gretel Bergmann, the high jumper? Well, she equalled the German record, but the moment that the Americans were on the boat to Berlin, Gretel received a letter telling her that she wasn't good enough for the German team.

And oh — I spoke to Jesse Owens only a few weeks back. And Jesse, he told me that he got the Big Hallo, tons of ticker tape, when he got back to New York, with his four gold medals. But he also told me that he wasn't allowed to enter his hotel by the front door. No, Jesse was black and he had to go in through the kitchen. And I have often thought, if sport had stood up and been counted, if America and other major nations had boycotted the Olympics, would it have made any difference? It might. After all, the Nazi Olympics, all eight million bucks of it, was the biggest national public relations venture in the history of the world. It was a major part of Hitler's Master Plan to revive the spirits of the nation, and any boycott would have been an immense blow to German pride.

So, would Hitler have been able to embark upon his conquest of Europe with the full backing of a confident Master Race? Would the Holocaust ever have taken place? We'll never know. The ifs of history stretch from here to Albuquerque. But what we DO know is that both our present and our future depend on what we do, what we are willing to sacrifice, for people who need our help, strangers we'll never meet. That we know for certain. That we know for sure.

Open up to see Germans and Americans working together to unload the planes. Drone of engines. Freeze.

Lights down.

The end.

ORWELL ON JURA

CHARACTERS

George Orwell, novelist and journalist; born Eric Arthur Blair
Mr McKinnon, Orwell's Jura landlord
Dr Williamson, consultant at Hairmyres Hospital
Fred Warburg, Orwell's publisher
Cyril Connolly, literary critic and writer
Dr Veraswami, a character in Orwell's *Burmese Days*
Danny Ibbotson, a character in Orwell's *Down the Mine*
Maria, a character in Orwell's *Homage to Catalonia*
Avril Blair, Orwell's sister
Boxer, a character in Orwell's *Animal Farm*
Winston Smith, the hero of Orwell's *1984*

Setting

A farmhouse on the remote island of Jura, off the west coast of Scotland, 1948.

Scene 1

Image of the island and shore. The sound of seagulls, wind, waves.

ORWELL   Fancy a spot of salmon fishing today, McKinnon?

MCKINNON   No' the day, Mr. Orwell, no' the day. It's ower rough, ower rough.

ORWELL   Rough? Bracing, I'd call it.

MCKINNON   Hiv it yer ain way, sur. Bit jist ye take care, jist ye have a mind.

ORWELL   Mind? Mind what?

MCKINNON   Corryvreckan, sur. That whirlpool. It's been the end of many a guid man in its time.

ORWELL   Then I won't go anywhere near your Corryvreckan, McKinnon. You have my word on it.

Image of the sea and Corryvreckan whirlpool, the sound of the sea gets louder, and the lights dim. Crossfade with soft sounds of a hospital.

Scene 2

Hairmires Hospital, East Kilbride.

WILLIAMSON So you have finally returned to us, Mr. Orwell.

ORWELL   Where in God's name am I?

WILLIAMSON Hairmires Hospital, East Kilbride, courtesy of Lord Astor, delivered to our care ten days ago in a Rolls Royce no less, but not a sensible word out of you since your arrival.

ORWELL   And who on earth would you be?

WILLIAMSON My name is Doctor Williamson. Mr. Orwell, you have been in and out of consciousness, in conference with the walls since you were first brought here to us, close to death. So yes, we have spoken, but I'm not at all certain that you will remember anything that we discussed.

ORWELL   What on earth happened to me?

WILLIAMSON Madness, madness on stilts. Because no man in his right mind would have ventured anywhere near the whirlpool of Corryvreckan on that day. Even someone like you, deprived of the benefit of a Scottish education should have known that.

ORWELL   I remember now. It all happened so quickly. Fishing with my son Richard — it had been absolutely marvellous — those salmon were speaking to me, they were literally flying on to my hook — then suddenly, without warning, we were both flailing about in the freezing water.

WILLIAMSON The pair of you were lucky to get back alive to the farmhouse. Together, you walked three miles back to Barnhill in the mud in bare feet, both soaked to the skin. Do you remember anything of that?

ORWELL No, not very much. Just strange dreams.

WILLIAMSON Your son, he appears to be a very robust young man, Mr. Orwell — strangely, he seems to have suffered no ill effects, but you...

ORWELL My lungs?

WILLIAMSON Tubercular, since 1937, according to your records. Your conduct that day was that of a raving lunatic, Mr. Orwell, even had you been a fit and healthy man, which you are most decidedly not.

ORWELL But I'm right as rain, Doctor — I contain multitudes.

WILLIAMSON Perhaps so, but everyone in your multitudes has tuberculosis in both lungs.

ORWELL Touché. Thanks for the sermon, Doctor. When can I get back to Jura — to my novel?

WILLIAMSON Mr. Orwell, let me be absolutely frank with you. When you first arrived, none of us here would have laid any bets on your survival. As I said, you have been delirious for almost a week, and very close to death. But a few days ago, the United States of America suddenly stepped in.

ORWELL The USA? What on earth did those Americans do?

WILLIAMSON Your friend Lord Astor clearly has some friends in high places. He secured for you through the American Embassy what they, in typical American parlance, describe as 'a new wonder drug'. This has been administered to you by injection over the past few days, and you have responded immediately and positively to it. Remarkable.

ORWELL   The Yanks. The cavalry — they always come to the rescue. So this drug, what on earth is it called?

WILLIAMSON Streptomycin.

ORWELL   Strepto what? Could you please spell it out for me, doctor?

WILLIAMSON S-t-r-e-p-t-o-m-y-c-i-n.

ORWELL   Amazing — I'm being cured by something that I can't even spell.

WILLIAMSON Well, it certainly seems to work, Mr. Orwell, though we don't yet know exactly why. But then, remember that all science is provisional.

ORWELL   All science is provisional — I think that I'll use that somewhere in an essay, Doctor, but don't expect any credit. It lines up with something that Arthur Koestler once said to me — he said that we learn nothing from science — no, we learn from experience.

WILLIAMSON Your Mr. Koestler may well have a valid point. So you have become almost overnight what might well be described as our national guinea pig.

ORWELL   So how on earth did you ever manage to work out the exact dosage?

WILLIAMSON Guesswork, pure guesswork.

ORWELL   That is a great comfort to me. So what you are now telling me is that my wonder drug could very well prove to be the death of me.

WILLIAMSON Unlikely, Mr. Orwell, but any drug of such potency is bound to produce side-effects. Memory-loss, hallucinations, swelling of the joints, that sort of thing.

ORWELL   So is that some other part of me is liable to fall off suddenly, without warning?

WILLIAMSON Probably — but no doubt Mr. Bevin's new-fangled Health Service, will soon put it back on again, Mr. Orwell.

ORWELL   So I've got those bloody Americans to thank. I'm surprised that Truman ever allowed it — he absolutely hated *Animal Farm*. He apparently thought that my pig Napoleon represented Josef Stalin.

WILLIAMSON As a matter of fact, so did I, Mr. Orwell. So did I.

ORWELL   Doctor Williamson, I wrote *Animal Farm* back in 1943, two years after Stalin had suddenly become saintly Uncle Joe, our country's best friend, not the slimy crook who had signed up with Adolf Hitler back in 1939. But then, suddenly the War was over and Uncle Joe the Commie became the Devil himself, so I suppose now he is the evil pig Napoleon, and I can get my wonder drug.

WILLIAMSON Just so. So if you will just sign here. This will give us the necessary formal permission to continue with your treatment. I must confess to you that your arrival has presented the Hospital with an excellent opportunity for experimenting with streptomycin.

ORWELL   And I represent the experiment?

WILLIAMSON Aye, that you do, sir. Without this drug, rest assured that we would almost certainly have been reading both of your obituaries by now, Mr. Orwell. You and Mr. Blair. That being said, we are, as your American friends might say, deep in Indian Country. Now to other equally serious issues which are of considerable concern to me. What good purpose, may I ask, does this serve? *(He holds up a small, leather bag.)*

ORWELL   That's my supply of loose tobacco, Doctor, for my cigarettes — I roll them myself.

WILLIAMSON That is not the answer to my question. Tell me — how many of these instruments of the Devil do you smoke per day?

ORWELL   Twenty, thirty, forty — what on earth does it matter?

WILLIAMSON With two tubercular lungs, it matters a great deal. An English friend of mine, Richard Doll, is now compiling statistics on the correlation between smoking and lung cancer. It already looks to Richard to be unarguable.

ORWELL   Correlations are not causes, Doctor.

WILLIAMSON A good point, but if I blindfold ten men and send them across a busy road, then ten men who are sighted, I rather think that cause and effect will take its natural course, and correlation and cause will be pretty much the same thing. If you continue on your present addiction to tobacco, you will for me represent the most stupid intelligent man within my medical experience.

ORWELL   I'll give what you have said some thought, Doctor Williamson, I solemnly promise you.

WILLIAMSON Excellent. So, with my expert advice ringing in your ears, you can return to your new novel, back to Jura in a few weeks, but not, I absolutely insist, anywhere near that whirlpool of Corryvreckan.

ORWELL   Point taken, Doctor. Anything else?

WILLIAMSON Yes, Mr. Orwell. My wife, Moyra, she adored *Animal Farm* — could you give her some idea of what your next novel is all about?

ORWELL   Let me try give you a wee clue, Doctor Williamson. Are you a film fan?

WILLIAMSON As a matter of fact, I am. And so is my wife.

ORWELL   Your clue is probably what is the best line in *The Wizard of Oz* — and it describes my next novel in a nutshell.

WILLIAMSON Mmmm. Let me think... aye, I may just have it.

ORWELL   You do?

WILLIAMSON Aye. *(Pause)* "Pay no attention to that man behind the curtain."

ORWELL   Good God! Doctor, you're absolutely right.

WILLIAMSON As I said before, never underestimate the value of a Scottish education, Mr. Orwell. Never, at the peril of your life.

ORWELL   My apologies, Doctor. I hardly imagined that Scottish education had reached as far as the works of L. Frank Baum.

WILLIAMSON It reaches as far as the eye can see, sir. It always has, it always will. But now a wee question for you. I hinted earlier that your treatment had produced some, shall we say, side-effects. One has been to engage in conversations with people we have been unable to locate. Who exactly is your Mr. McKinnon?

ORWELL   Have you got a few moments, Doctor?

WILLIAMSON Of course.

ORWELL   Then let me take you back to my first morning in Jura. And to the ethics of porridge.

Scene 3

Barnhill farmhouse.

Image of Barnhill farmhouse and 1946 appear on the screen.

Early morning. There is knocking on a door. Orwell rises as if from the bed in Barnhill to answer it.

ORWELL   Yes? *(The knocking resumes.)* Yes?

A bearded crofter in his early 60s enters nervously, holding in front of him a large covered plate.

MCKINNON *(Uncertain)* Sir... Mister?

ORWELL   Good morning — you'll be my landlord, Mr. McKinnon.

MCKINNON Aye, that's the plain truth of it, sur. *(Pause)* Aye. So... whit, whit do ye want me to call ye... mister...?

ORWELL   What do I want to be called? What on earth do you mean?

MCKINNON Ah mean, should ah call ye Mr. Blair or Mr. Orwell?

Orwell lifts the typewriter and places it on a table in the middle of the room.

ORWELL   To tell the truth, up till this moment I hadn't really given the matter much in the way of thought. So let's just turn the tables. Which name would you choose — if you were me?

MCKINNON   Sur, with a name like Cody McKinnon, ah'm no sure that ah'm qualified tae express an opinion.

ORWELL   Cody — where on earth did you get a name like Cody?

MCKINNON   Ma mother, back in 1892, she was at the Wild West Show doon in Glasgow, and she met the great Buffalo Bill Cody.

ORWELL   Just as well she didn't meet Sitting Bull.

MCKINNON   Aye, but ah'm the only Cody on the island, sur.

ORWELL   In Europe, I would reckon. But leaving that accident of nature to the side for a moment, which name would you choose for me, Orwell or Blair?

MCKINNON   Ah think Orwell, sur. It sounds more... more distinguished. Sort of upper class. Like the lairds.

ORWELL   Then it's all settled, Mr. McKinnon. It will be Orwell the laird, from this moment on. *(He coughs, a racking cough.)*

MCKINNON   This is for you, sir.

McKinnon timidly hands over the plate. Orwell goes to the table, lifts the top plate and holds the bottom plate up for examination. He shakes his head and lays it down on the table.

MCKINNON   Yer porridge, Mr. Orwell. Ma wife, Morag, she's made enough to last ye till the end o' the week, till yer sister comes up here tae tak' care of you.

ORWELL   Mmm. I must admit, McKinnon, that I have never encountered porridge quite like this before. It... it seems to be a sort of solid block.

MCKINNON   Aye, aye. Ye cut it up intae slices, Mr. Orwell, jist like bread, ye see. Then a' ye have tae do is tae add the hot water, and Bob's yer uncle, ye've got yer porridge. But jist one thing...

ORWELL   Yes?

MCKINNON   Dae ye tak' yer porridge Scots style or English style, Mr. Orwell?

ORWELL   Scots style — and what exactly would that be?

MCKINNON   Scots style is aye salted, Mr. Orwell. Salted. The lairds, the English, they aye tak' it with sugar. Sugar and mibbe even honey.

ORWELL   And what you're telling me, if I understand you correctly, is that sugar isn't right, that's not the way it ought to be. And that honey, I suppose that qualifies as nothing less than sheer decadence.

MCKINNON   That's no' really for me to say, sur.

ORWELL   Then salt it shall be, then, from this day forward, and I will rely on the good Mrs Morag McKinnon to insert exactly the right amount, lest I'm ever tempted to fall back into my evil English ways. *(McKinnon moves away from the table and hovers uncertainly.)* Is there anything else that you think I should know? I mean of a strictly ethical nature? Like the salt?

MCKINNON   Ah think yer making fun o' me, sur.

ORWELL   Quite right — that was just that other fellow Blair sounding off, like an English toff.

MCKINNON   Ma wife will come up here every Monday morn, Mr. Orwell, and bring ye up some hot water for yer bath.

ORWELL   Only once a week?

MCKINNON   Mr. Orwell, that's mair baths than most folks roond here tak' for the hale winter. No, up here we jist sow ourselves inta oor claes in October and then thole it out till May.

ORWELL   Well, Mr. McKinnon, I'm afraid that tholing will be a local custom that I may well be tempted to forego. Anything else?

MCKINNON   Well, ma wife, she's been asking me since we first let oot the place tae ye, and ah told her that ye wrote novels...

ORWELL   Yes?

MCKINNON   It's no matter tae me, mind, but ma Morag, she's dead set against anything that's how do ye say...

ORWELL   Racy?

MCKINNON   Aye. We're Wee Frees here, Mr. Orwell.

ORWELL   Yes. The Wee Frees. They tell me that you aren't even allowed to travel on Sundays.

MCKINNON   Aye. Or read anything save the Bible. The Lord's Day, sur. The day of rest. But yer novels...

ORWELL   No, McKinnon, I can assure you that there is nothing remotely racy in any of my novels, I'm afraid. Wish to hell there was, might well secure me better advances from my publisher. If you don't mind me asking — how many children do you have?

MCKINNON   Seven, sur.

ORWELL   Then you clearly have a wealth of practical knowledge in that element of human conduct that I do not, alas, possess. You see, I only write about what I know, and that hasn't been an area in which I have had any great quality of experience, more's the pity. Wish to God I had. *(Coughs)* Too late now, I'm afraid. No, McKinnon, I'm busy writing about the future, before the present finally catches up with me. *(Coughs)* The future. About forty years on. The way things might turn out to be.

MCKINNON   The future. Grand.

ORWELL   You haven't seen what I've written, my friend.

MCKINNON   But nothing...

ORWELL   No, nothing remotely sexual, and if I'm ever tempted to do so, rest assured I'll seek you out for counsel. *(Pause)* but before you go — have you any religious objection to my heating up your wife's porridge on a Sunday — a sort of heresy by proxy, so to speak?

MCKINNON   No, sur, it dinna apply to the English. Jist tae us, the Wee Frees.

ORWELL   Good. So please thank Mrs. McKinnon for me, and tell her to make sure to get the right amount of salt, just so I can sustain the strength to stay on the straight and narrow.

McKinnon salutes and leaves. Orwell takes the plate from the table, sits on his bed and surveys the porridge in front of him.

ORWELL   Wee, but hardly free.

Scene 4

1948. A plush Gentleman's Club, London. Soft sounds of the club etc. The publisher Fred Warburg and the writer Cyril Connolly are enjoying a drink.

FRED   I can't for the life of me understand why Eric couldn't just have parked himself in a comfy little bed and breakfast over in Great Yarmouth, Cyril, to write this novel of his.

CYRIL   Hardship, Mister Publisher. Eric absolutely revels in hardship.

FRED   Eton, he was with you at Eton, Cyril — that's probably where he first embraced the Spartan life. The Wall Game, all that mud.

CYRIL   Probably. So now he is on God-forsaken Jura and a farmhouse by the name of Barnhill, courtesy of Lord Astor, with no hot water and no electricity.

FRED   No. Just the malt whisky to keep him warm. Glenmorangie, from recent memory.

CYRIL   But come on — didn't you give him an absolutely whopping advance? Two hundred pounds?

FRED   Three hundred.

CYRIL   Three hundred pounds! Eric could have parked himself at the Ritz on that kind of money. He must have some Calvinistic Scotch blood in him.

FRED   I thought that he didn't like the Scots.

CYRIL   No, he doesn't. He thinks they tend to be a bit too... too Scottish. All those cabers and bagpipes. So maybe the Scots, that's just another part of the punishment.

FRED   Punishment for what, God help us?

CYRIL   Almost certainly simply for being alive, but more likely for not having done enough. Eric always seems to think that he hasn't done enough. Yes, I seem to remember that he once told me that he had plans to turn the Home Guard into a sort of civilian national militia, after the War.

FRED   Come on, you've just made that up.

CYRIL   No. Cross my heart and hope to die. *(Pause)* By now, he'll be tapping away with his index finger on that creaky old Remington...

FRED   Puffing away on one of his wretched roll-ups.

CYRIL   And coughing fit to burst. Eric's not well, you know. He never has been — even before he was wounded in Spain in the Civil War.

FRED   I asked him about that a few months ago, when he came over for a drink. Do you know what he said to me? He said that he had been disappointed that he hadn't felt any pain when that bullet hit him.

CYRIL   That's typical Eric. *(Pause)* So come on, what's this new book of his all about? Hard Times over at the BBC?

FRED   No, he hated it at the Beeb — a tyranny of mediocrities he called it. Too much censorship.

CYRIL   No way round it, Fred. Not back then. The War. The BBC, it had a bounden duty to keep up the national morale against the Boche.

FRED   Yes, using our precious arts as a sort of club, to beat Adolf Hitler. Did you know, Eric once told me that when the Huns were besieging Leningrad and Prokoviev was conducting the first performance of his Leningrad Concerto, the German troops heard it on the radio. And do you know what the buggers did?

CYRIL   Shelled the concert hall.

FRED   How on earth did you know that?

CYRIL   Because, my dear friend, like our man in far-off Jura, I am the repository of a fund of useless knowledge. But let's get back to our man Eric's next novel. You haven't answered my question — what's it all about?

FRED   It's all very hush-hush, Cyril. Hoosh hoosh. But I am allowed to reveal to you that it's all set some time in the future. Dystopian.

CYRIL   Science fiction? *A Brave New World* kind of thing?

FRED   Grave New World, if I know anything about our Eric. No, I'm not absolutely certain, but I've asked him to take a low profile on the politics this time around.

CYRIL   Yes, we don't want another *Animal*-bloody-*Farm* debate. Can't make any sense of those lawyers, how any politician could possibly see himself in the book as an animal.

FRED   What about a pig?

CYRIL   Point taken. But his *Animal Farm*, it's made him a helluva lot of enemies on the Left, you know.

FRED   Yes, and that's why Eric will sleep every night with a Luger under his pillow.

CYRIL   What on earth for?

FRED   *Animal Farm*. He thinks that the Russians might well try to bump him off.

CYRIL   You mean like Trotsky?

FRED   Yes. Our Eric may at this point be suffering from a slight touch of *folie de grandeur*, Cyril.

CYRIL   In spades.

FRED   But it doesn't stop there. He phoned me a couple of weeks ago, saying some drugs are starting to give him strange dreams, hallucinations.

CYRIL   What sort of thing?

FRED   The past. People keep arriving from his past.

CYRIL   I get them all the time. Trouble is, I always seem to owe them money.

FRED   No — going back to his writing, even in *Animal Farm*, Eric has always drawn from reality, from something that has happened to him, or to someone else that he knows.

CYRIL   I thought that was what fiction was all about.

FRED   You know what I mean, Cyril.

CYRIL   Real, but not so real that we can actually recognise them.

FRED   Tell me, you've known him for a lifetime, what makes him tick?

CYRIL   Correction, Fred, correction. Yes, we've been friends for a lifetime. But I haven't known Eric for a minute.

Scene 5

Orwell sits at his desk, on his right side on the desk a compact pile of pristine white paper, on the typewriter in front of him a furled, untouched sheet. On the three walls there are side-on slides of him, poised at his typewriter, just as he is now. He has a pile of screwed-up little bundles of white paper on the table on his left, rejected first pages. He types for a few moments, surveys his work, then pulls out the sheet, screws it up, lays it with the others, and groans. Orwell walks to a waste paper basket a few feet away and draws it closer to his table. He picks up a little bundle and throws it easily into the basket. Good. He moves the basket further away, and throws again, successfully. He grins, and moves it much further away.

ORWELL   The Olympic Games — round one. Orwell, Great Britain. *(He throws again and again, until he succeeds)* First-round leader — Orwell, Great Britain, distance, three metres sixteen centimetres. *(He returns to his typewriter and taps away for a few seconds, then shakes his head in despair.)* I suppose nothing can ever go well that begins with getting up in the morning. And even worse when that morning starts with trying to find the first line of a novel, begging it, imploring it to come from somewhere, anywhere, into your empty head, and then on to that terrible blank page.

Winnie the Pooh, here is the first line, "Once upon a time, a very long time ago now, about last Friday" that was it, the first line — I wonder how many days, months, years it took Milne to find it, or did that line somehow immediately float out of the ether and find HIM? We'll never know, because authors are a weird bunch — they rarely discuss how they write their novels, and even if they did, they would describe so many completely different ways that we would end up even more confused than when we started.

The American, Robert Benchley, do you know that he once spent all day with nothing on the page except a single word? It was "the" T.H.E. THE. He then got up, went out and had a few drinks with some of his buddies at the Algonquin Hotel. Then, refreshed by this, when he thought that he had pulled himself together, he went back to his typewriter, and added three more words to his "the" first line — they were " hell with it!"

I am not by nature a religious man, but God, I think that he got it absolutely right — just look at those first lines in the Bible "In the Beginning was the Word, and the Word is with God and the Word was God". Got you!

And God, he might well have written, "when you hold a man by the balls, then his heart and mind will surely follow." Because that is really what a novel is all about, grabbing the reader's attention, and holding on to it, page by page by page. You can always write later chapters where things slow up a bit, because by that time the reader is in the palm of your hand — you have hooked him, and he is your prisoner for the rest of the journey.

But it has been all day and it still isn't coming through, it hasn't found me yet, but it has to, it bloody-well must. It's usually like a dam bursting — once you get that first line, you are carried along by the flow, and before you know where you are, you are twenty pages in, and it's all simply pouring out of you, as if it had already been there, just waiting to get on the page. Which, of course, it never was.

And my title, that doesn't help. I've never been very good at titles — *Burmese Days*, *Keep the Aspidistra Flying*, hardly titles calculated to set the blood racing. *The Last Man in Europe*, that's my best attempt, as things stand at the moment.

Orwell's hands hang above the typewriter. He types, reads, shakes his head, pulls out the sheet, crunches it up, throws it away, missing the wastepaper basket. He shakes his head.

ORWELL   No, no, it simply won't come. Perhaps I should just go out and work for a bit on my patch of Jersey Royals — the first to be grown in the Hebrides — no, let's us just try again. *Nil desperandum.*

Maybe, maybe this lack of confidence all goes back to when I was a child, this insecurity. For I was a thoroughly obnoxious little boy, constantly into all sorts of mischief always being sent to the headmaster for a beating.

My younger sister Avril, once she found me alone in the garden, standing on my head, and she asked me why. I answered because it was the best way of getting attention. Attention — the only attention that I ever got from my father was the word DON'T, and my mother, she seemed to exist in some sweet parallel world of her own. It would have taken a ouija board to make contact with her.

So I simply lived my life deep in my head, then somehow from somewhere I got the idea that I was ugly, and that feeling, it lodged with me, like an unwelcome guest, for many years. Even in my four years at Eton, my literary ambitions were very much mixed up with this feeling of being unwanted, of being alone in my head. But from the very start, I knew that I had a good feeling for words, and even more important, I had the capacity to face unpleasant facts. But now the immediate unpleasant fact is that I don't have a first line, and perhaps, perhaps it's time now for yet another row of pills... and bed. *(He reaches for the whisky and pours a glass, moves the pill boxes towards him.)*

The lights dim, as they come up again Orwell is at the table, typewriter in front of him, dozing, head on table. Behind him a Burmese gentleman, Dr Veraswami, enters, and stands, still.

VERASWAMI Please give the bearer fifteen lashes.

Orwell shakes his head and looks drunkenly around him.

ORWELL   What?

VERASWAMI Please give the bearer fifteen lashes. You told me that is what they always used to say, back in the old days of the Empire. That was the standard punishment for a native servant, as I remember you telling me.

ORWELL   Doctor Veraswami! What in God's name are you doing here, my dear fellow? Yes, you're right, that's what that oaf Lackersteen used to say down at the club, day in day out. The old days. Fifteen lashes.

VERASWAMI Yes, that is what you told me. The golden days of the Raj.

ORWELL   The Raj, the Raj. Let me just try to collect my thoughts, old friend. Yes, I've got it now. But you, my dear doctor, you do not exist.

VERASWAMI Of course I do, my dear Mr. Orwell. I am your creation. You created me. So I will always exist.

ORWELL   Yes. *Burmese Days.* So now I suppose I've got to play the part of the hero, Clary, the one with the birthmark?

VERASWAMI Yes, my friend, you could very well be. But as I remember it, you killed him off, in your final chapter.

ORWELL   But don't forget, my dear Veraswami, Orwell is a fiction too.

VERASWAMI Fact, fiction — I recollect that you once said to me, who knows where one ends and the other begins?

ORWELL   Touché. Couldn't have put it better. So how are you now, my dear fellow?

VERASWAMI Alas, exactly as you left me, my friend. Sadly, I was never accepted as a member of the European club.

ORWELL   Lucky you.

VERASWAMI No, my dear Orwell. Membership of the European club would have, as you might say, represented the absolute pinnacle of my existence.

ORWELL   Some pinnacle! Dogs, gramophones, dog-eared *Punch* magazines and tennis racquets. And always fulminating about natives and Mongolian brothers, always droning endlessly on about the Good Old Days, and how the Empire was going to the dogs. Always made me want to throw up.

VERASWAMI But my dear friend, what on earth has made you so cynical? You — an Englishman of such undoubted quality of character? Uttering sentiments of sedition that might well have come out of that radical paper *The Burmese Patriot*?

ORWELL   Don't you see? Don't you see? I... we were only in Burma to make money, Veraswami. So no, I didn't want you to drive us out of Burma — that would have meant that I would have lost my job. No, what I took exception to, what I loathed was all this slimy White Man's Burden garbage. Being the Pukka Sahib. Living the Great Lie.

VERASWAMI But what lie, Mr. Orwell? What lie?

ORWELL   The old lie, the ancient lie, my friend. That we had come all the way to Burma to help our black brothers, when we were really only there to rob you blind. If only we had been honest and admitted — even privately — that we were bloody thieves, and then go about our thieving without all this humbug, all this wretched hypocrisy.

VERASWAMI But my dear Mr. Orwell, you were not thieves, no, the English, you were our benefactors.

ORWELL   Doctor, our glorious British Empire was simply a device to deliver trade monopolies to the English, or rather to gangs of Jews and Scotchmen.

VERASWAMI But please reflect for a moment... Burma would have been quite helpless without you. For, my dear friend, you quite forget the essentially weak nature of our character. The English, you brought us law and order. *Pax Brittanica.*

ORWELL   Pox Brittanica, more like. Venereal diseases by the dozen.

VERASWAMI No, my friend, these plagues were brought to Burma by the filthy Orientals and the Chinese. Such people, they were the ones who brought the diseases, and the English, with their medical science, they were the ones who cured them. That is the way of the British Empire.

ORWELL   All of this is so *déjà vu*, my dear doctor. We've had this identical conversation so many times, old fellow.

VERASWAMI And always, always I have enjoyed it immensely, Mr. Orwell. The sharp cut and thrust of debate, you always called it, as I remember. So very English.

ORWELL   Yes. So necessary and so absolutely bloody pointless.

VERASWAMI What you fail to see, my friend, is that your civilisation, even at its worst, represented for us in Burma a distinct advance. Gramophones, billycock hats, even the *News of the World*, all of these were vastly superior to the ghastly sloth of the Oriental.

ORWELL   My dear doctor, I can see that this a subject on which we will never, ever reach agreement. The truth is you like all this modern progress, while my view is, shall we say, somewhat more jaundiced. So if the English were indeed a civilising influence, it was really only so that we could grab from you on a larger scale. If it hadn't paid, we would soon have given up and left you all to rot.

VERASWAMI Mr. Orwell, please, I beg you, cast all such dreadful thoughts from your mind. If you truly disapproved of the British

Empire, you would not merely have said so privately to me. No, you would have stood up and proclaimed it loudly from the pulpit. I think that I know you, Mr. Orwell, perhaps even better than you know yourself.

ORWELL   Proclaiming from the pulpit? Sorry, my dear doctor, I simply didn't have the balls for anything like that. No, back then, you had to be the perfect pukka sahib or else be cast into the Outer Darkness.

VERASWAMI So why do you have me now come here to you and then say such terrible things to me?

ORWELL   Because, my dear friend, my dear Doctor Veraswami, you were — you still are — my precious safety valve, my Black Mass on the sly. I know that I can say absolutely anything to you, dear friend.

VERASWAMI Mr. Orwell, sometimes I used to think that you said all these things only to — what is the term? — to pull my leg. The famous English sense of humour. We natives, we possess no such humour, that is an accepted fact.

ORWELL   Lucky devils. Our famous sense of humour, that and the good old stiff upper lip — it's been the bloody death of us.

VERASWAMI I can see that we will never, ever agree, Mr Orwell. But let me leave and say that it has been a pleasure, sir, to meet and converse with you again. I wish you well. Goodbye. *(He leaves.)*

ORWELL   Veraswami! Veraswami! Come back, come back. You're the only one that I can bloody well talk to! Come back!

Scene 6

ORWELL   OK, so I might as well come clean now, though it's clear as the nose on your face. Pretty much everything that I have written so far has been all about me, me, me. The plain fact is that I'm not very good at getting into the minds and the feelings of other people.

So in *Burmese Days,* I gave my hero Clary a birthmark on his cheek — a bit of subconscious symbolism there, probably, but Clary is me, me without the pen, me without the typewriter, me dead come to that. And this has led all the way from Burma to Jura, now and Winston Smith, who is really Clary without the birthmark.

Of course, I knew from the moment that I arrived in Burma as a policeman in the Colonial Service, responsible for 200,000 lesser breeds without the Law, that me, I was simply a small part of what was nothing less than a massive Imperial fraud. And I knew, I knew right from the start that I would never ever be one of them, one of that braying, pompous bunch of frauds.

But deep down, what always bothered me, I also knew that, given time, I would have grown to become a part of that fraud and that always nagged away at me. For even a dead fish can float with the current, downstream, but it takes a live one to swim against it. And that is what I set myself to do when I returned to England's green and pleasant land. *(He starts to type, coughing away. He stops.)* No, no, it won't bloody well come. So it's back to the malt.

Scene 7

Total darkness. A spotlight on the image of a painting of blackened miner in miner's gear. Danny enters.

MINER   "Blackened to the eyes, with their throats full of coal dust, driving their shovels forward with arms and belly muscles full of steel", that's what you said — I read it in your book, Mr. Orwell.

Light on Orwell in bed. He gets up, sits on the bed, rubbing his eyes.

ORWELL   Danny — if it's not Danny Ibbotson!

DANNY   You remembered my name, Mr. Orwell!

ORWELL   How in God's name could I ever forget it? I would have died down there in that bloody mine without you, Danny.

DANNY   No, not you Mr. Orwell, no, never, never in a month of Sundays.

ORWELL   Danny, dear innocent soul that I was, I thought that you simply walked down some sort of a tunnel, dug out the bloody coal and put it in sacks.

DANNY   Not drop at fifty miles an hour in a lift with ten men pissing their pants with fear, and then walk two miles to the seam.

ORWELL   Walk? That two miles — it took me over an hour and a half, all hunched up like Quasimodo, or crawling on my bloody hands and knees.

DANNY   It was all of two hours. You slowed us all up that morning, Mr. Orwell, 'cos forty minutes, that was our normal time. Then it was eight hours hacking away at the seam, and forty minutes back .

ORWELL   And, as I remember it, your walk to the seam didn't actually count as work — you only got paid for the coal that you dug, not the time you spent down there in the hellish hole. Sixteen tons a day, naked, hacking away at that wretched seam. And with all those bloody rats scuttling over your feet.

DANNY   Bread and dripping and cold tea.

ORWELL   And none of the luxuries of modern hygiene.

DANNY   None at all.

ORWELL   But hold on, hold on. You've changed Danny — for the moment, I can't quite put my finger on it — but somehow you've changed. I've got it — you don't speak the way you used to.

DANNY   Don't I? Well, that was because of you, Mr. Orwell.

ORWELL   How?

DANNY   Do you remember that you said that you liked my paintings? Yorkshire primitive, you called them?

ORWELL   Yes — they were very good indeed. I still have the one that you gave me, it's hanging in my lounge as we speak.

DANNY   But do you remember, you gave me five pounds for art lessons in Bradford, but I went and put the money on a bet with our local bookie, at ten to one.

ORWELL   Those are big odds, Danny — was it on a greyhound?

DANNY   No. The money was on you, Mr. Orwell. You see, no one thought that you would ever make it out to the seam — you're far too tall, and you'd never done a hard day's work in your life. So I picked up fifty pounds on you, six months wages.

ORWELL   Good for you, Danny. Good for you.

DANNY   No, good for you. But that's not where it ends, Mr. Orwell. The same bookie gave forty to one against you making it both ways, and I put my week's wages on that. Two quid.

ORWELL   So it was another eighty pounds when I made it back.

DANNY   A hundred and forty pounds in all. That took me out of the pit for good, and to my first year at art college. Then I got me a scholarship for the next two years, and took my diploma. Next it was the War, and a commission in the Army Educational Corps.

ORWELL   Good on you, Danny. Good on you. So you are a painter now — what do you paint?

DANNY   Miners, Mr. Orwell. Miners.

He exits, the lights dip and come up again.

ORWELL   They all call me a leftie, and yes, I suppose that's what I have always been, a supporter of the working classes, but then so is my publisher, Fred Warburg, so is dear old George Bernard Shaw, but to people like them, to them the working classes exist only in the abstract. For neither of them have ever done a hard day's physical work in their lives, and never will, neither of them have ever been on the dole, neither of them have ever seen first-hand what actually happens in a Lancashire cotton mill, and neither of them would have lasted five minutes down a coal mine.

And that was why, back in 1933, I decided to find out what it was really like to be at the bottom of the heap, what it was like to sweat your guts out every day for bugger all, and years later what it was like to drop at fifty miles an hour into a smelly hell hole and hack away at a seam of coal, with mice and rats scuttling about your feet for ten hours a day.

And so first off, I went to Paris. There, in a smelly little flat, I lived with a White Russian by the name of Boris — I don't think that I ever did discover his second name. Boris sported — though that's probably the wrong word — Boris sported a bulbous stomach, big enough to merit its own postcode. I well remember that one week we were so poor that we couldn't afford to buy any food at all. But the strange thing was that Boris' stomach somehow defied the laws of physics, because it remained at exactly the same size. I once suggested to him that he leave his body to science, but now, on reflection, I rather think that Boris should have left it to science fiction.

Then we both got a job in the kitchens of a big Paris hotel, up to our elbows in lukewarm, greasy dishwater for twelve hours a day. But the first day on the job, the left-overs, the left-overs, they were an absolute joy. But then, that same first week, Marcel, the little weasel who had got Boris and I our jobs at the hotel in the first place, he ran off with the few centimes that I had earned from all those hours of dishwashing, so I was left with absolutely nothing.

Next, I ended up sick as a dog with pneumonia in a dreadful Paris hospital, and that was where I first learnt what it was like to be at the bottom of the pile, in France, in a bed in the charity ward. For suddenly you became absolutely nothing, simply a few kilos of decaying meat to be inspected and prodded and injected, while all around you the other inmates were begging for a pissoir or being subjected to a bizarre treatment called cupping. This was a medieval practice which involved placing hot glasses on your skin, drawing forth bubbles of flesh, then piercing them with long needles and withdrawing fluids. Hideous.

But somehow, somehow I survived. You know, I am now of the firm conviction that the English public school provides the perfect experience in strengthening a man's will to survive. Thus, I arrived back in England, ready to drop even further down the social ladder, by becoming a tramp, wandering from spike to spike.

And what, I can hear you ask, is a spike? A spike is about as low as any man can get, a state lodging house for men at the bottom of the heap, beggars who have absolutely nothing. But right away, right away I found that, if anything could save you from the ministrations of the Tramp Major, he was the brutal Gauleiter who ran the spike, it was your accent. For the Tramp Major, the moment that I opened my mouth, realised that I was not like the others, the detritus who infested his Kingdom, no, I was a gent, so I was treated differently, and was given a cushy job in the kitchen.

It was winter, and it was like hell on earth, no not like hell, for at least hell would have been warm. Thus, forty half-naked, smelly cadaverous creatures were crowded into the same room for twelve hours a day, fed bread and weak tea, then dumped in cells for the night by the Tramp Major, before being sent off to the next awful Spike.

I say that I became *Down and Out in Paris and London* to find out what it was like to be poor, to be at the bottom of the heap, but no, that's not completely true. For I experienced only what it was LIKE to be poor, not what it WAS to be poor, for that was impossible, because for these men this was it — trudging from spike to spike forever, all the way to a pauper's grave but no, not for me. For me it was simply part of a little drama which I would soon bring to the nation's attention in my writing. Me, I always had something, someone to go back to. These men, they had absolutely nothing.

Because I had taken a quite different route from those sorry lost souls, one that would always keep me separate from them, separate indeed from everyone except those of my own class. And even now, in this bright new dawn of a Labour Government, though the Heart of England may have changed, its balls remain resolutely in the same place, on the playing fields of Eton.

There is a soft strum of guitars, a Spanish woman in mannish clothes comes in quietly behind him and covers his eyes. She is smoking(?)

ORWELL   Maria. Maria del Monte! I was wondering when you might choose to make an appearance.

MARIA   How... how did you know it was me?

ORWELL   It was the *Gauloise*, Maria, the *Gauloise*. I will never for the life of me forget that ghastly smell.

MARIA   My beloved *Gauloise*. Do you remember when I was down to only one a day?

ORWELL   Yes, in those awful trenches, way up in the frozen mountains, in November of 1935. As I remember it, you were absolutely insufferable.

MARIA   A pain in the arse was what you called me then.

ORWELL   Yes, I remember that I was always given to understatement.

MARIA   One *Gauloise* a day. However did I manage to survive?

ORWELL   I did offer you one of my roll-ups.

MARIA   Yes, you did, but it came to pieces in my hands.

ORWELL   It came from a delicate plant, Maria.

MARIA   Eric, I have often asked myself — why did you ever come to Spain to help us fight the Fascists?

ORWELL   Because, because and I know that this will sound lame to you, it seemed to be the right thing to do at the time.

MARIA   And your wife?

ORWELL   Dear sweet, trusting Eileen. Thank God she didn't come up with me into the mountains. We didn't really have a clue, either of us, of what we were getting into, coming to Spain, to fight Fascism. None of us English really did.

MARIA   Too many American movies, Eric. Goodies versus baddies.

ORWELL   And how on earth were we to know that we had so many baddies on our own side?

MARIA   We were naïve, my dear Eric. Naïve.

ORWELL   Eric. Not many people call me Eric anymore.

MARIA   No, it's George Orwell now. The pen is mightier than the sword.

ORWELL   It's not either or, my dear Maria. Without the sword...

MARIA   It was a Mauser rifle, Eric.

ORWELL   Yes, I remember, a totally useless 1893 Mauser. Always jamming. About as much use as a chocolate teapot.

MARIA   Yes, they were always falling apart. Those Mausers must have killed as many of us as it did of them.

ORWELL   Yes, but remember if it hadn't been for that clapped out old Mauser, I would never have had the slightest notion of what war was all about.

MARIA   To be under fire.

ORWELL   And to return fire, even though I couldn't hit the ground with my hat.

MARIA   But always with the best intentions, Eric.

ORWELL   With which the road to hell is so liberally paved.

MARIA   The people versus Fascism. Who could have known that Hitler's best friend would turn out to be none other than Josef Stalin?

ORWELL   Who knew about as much about Spain as he did about Chorlton-cum-Hardy?

MARIA   It was war by proxy. And you took a bullet for it.

ORWELL   Yes I did. Do you know the best thing about those months in the mountains, Maria?

MARIA   No.

ORWELL   It was those steaming mugs of tea that you used to serve up, Maria. Glorious, marvellous.

MARIA   Yes, Eric... that tea... I have a confession to make...

ORWELL   You mean that it wasn't you who made the tea?

MARIA   No. I made it.

ORWELL   Well, what, then?

MARIA   It wasn't tea, Eric. We ran out of tea at the end of that first month.

ORWELL   But it was a magnificent brew. What was it then?

MARIA   Wood, Eric, it was wood.

ORWELL   Wood? Maria, are you are now here telling me, after all these years, that I was drinking wood?

MARIA   Yes, you were. My mother, we were poor people, we couldn't afford tea, so she had always used a root, which she broke it down into a powder. I found that root, ground it down and put it into empty tea bags.

ORWELL   I must have drunk about a hundred gallons of that wood, Maria, in those months before I got shot. No wonder I survived — the bullet must have hit a branch.

MARIA   Do you think that I should have kept this all to myself?

ORWELL   Not really. It's a sort of liquid testimony to the body's capacity for survival, living off wood and rolled-up cigarettes that disintegrated in your hands.

MARIA   One question, Eric, before I go. *(Pause)* Why didn't you ever try to make love to me?

ORWELL   Well, I can't say that I didn't consider it, from time to time.

MARIA   Then, why not?

ORWELL   I really didn't think that you would be interested.

MARIA   I was — if only for comfort.

ORWELL   Comfort — that's a good way of putting it, Maria. No, I was too shy. But it's nice to know that you thought about me in that way.

MARIA   I did — and often.

ORWELL   But you didn't give me any clues, Maria. A man like me, at that point in my life, I always needed some clues.

MARIA   What about that time that you helped me out of the mud? When you held my hand?

ORWELL   What about it?

MARIA   Didn't you feel it, Eric, the pressure?

ORWELL   No, Maria, I didn't.

MARIA   And what about that time when I kissed you on the mouth?

ORWELL   I remember, I had cut my hand on that wretched Mauser, and you bandaged it all up for me.

MARIA   Yes.

ORWELL   Maria, I must freely admit — that moment did give me pause.

MARIA   But you did nothing.

ORWELL   No. Too English.

MARIA   Stiff upper lip.

ORWELL   Yes. Quite literally.

MARIA   A pity — it might have been a comfort.

ORWELL *(coughs)* Maria, why are you here?

MARIA   To thank you — after all, you are still on the wanted list in Spain, and you took a bullet for us.

ORWELL   And took it, quite literally, in the neck.

MARIA   And to ask you... was it all worth it?

ORWELL   Yes, because it was an education for me, being in the trenches, rather than merely writing about war sitting behind a desk. And you?

MARIA   Yes, but next time I will come better prepared.

ORWELL   How?

MARIA   First, that I stack up with a crate of *Gauloise* before a single shot is fired.

ORWELL   And second?

MARIA   A Kalashnikov rifle, and a thousand bullets.

ORWELL   So how did it go with you, after I went off to hospital?

MARIA   Not so good, Eric, not so good. First, it was off to France where I ran a brothel for sailors in Toulouse. Then there was the Resistance, that... that was much better. *(Pause)* At least until the Gestapo caught up with me in 1943. *(Pause)* I must go now, Eric. *(She moves towards the door.)*

ORWELL   Jolly good of you to visit me, Maria. I always thought that you were dead.

MARIA   I am, Eric. I am.

She exits as the lights change.

Orwell pours a scotch, reaches for his cigarettes and moves around restlessly.

ORWELL   Do you know what I remember most about the Spanish Civil War? No, it wasn't getting that wretched bullet in the neck, though I'm never going to forget that, no, what I remember most clearly, most vividly was the dreadful smell.

You see, in the Spanish type of latrine — the Spaniards must have completely different excretory mechanisms from the Anglo-Saxon — you had to squat and make your deposit into a hole in the floor. And that Spanish floor, it was made of some strange kind of polished stone. And, and it meant that when you decided to make your effort, you almost invariably lost your balance, and slid all over the place. So, just to try to get some fun out of it, I used to award myself marks out of ten for what might best be called excretory accuracy. As I remember it, my best was a couple of eights, but when I was constipated I was down to threes and fours, and sliding all over the place.

The description of the Spanish Civil War which I presented when I wrote *Homage to Catalonia*, it's substantially true. Bullets hurt, corpses stink and men under fire are often so frightened that they wet their trousers. That's the way it was. That's the way that it will always be. People tend to forget that a soldier on duty anywhere near the line is usually too hungry, too frightened to bother about how he ever got there, or about the political origins of his war. So, whatever the justice of your cause, a louse is still a louse, and a bomb is still a bomb.

For over twenty years, the Left had jeered at the "glory" of war, at atrocity stories, at patriotism, even, God help me, at physical courage. Well, in 1937, the very same people were denouncing you as a Trotskyist if you denied the stories that wounded men were clamouring to get back into the fight. The hell they were.

Let me tell you a little story. Early one morning, I went out to do a bit of sniping with my old Mauser 93. I remember waiting on the edge of the woods for hours, simply to get a shot at somebody, anybody. Then, suddenly, I see this skinny little Fascist fellow, clearly carrying some sort of a message on a clipboard, running half-dressed, across a parapet, holding up his trousers with his left hand. It would've been easy but I didn't take a shot at him. Why not? Because the poor little bugger was holding up his trousers. I had come to Huesca to kill Fascists, not to shoot at some wretch who was struggling to retain what remained of his manly dignity. At that moment, he ceased being a Fascist, he was simply a fellow human being and I couldn't pull the trigger.

And anyhow, later I discovered in war it took on average a thousand bullets to kill a single man. I worked it out, that by that measure, it would have taken me at least twenty years to kill a single fascist.

In early life I had realised that no event is ever correctly reported in a newspaper, and Spain, that was no different. So there, I saw great battles reported when there had been no fighting at all, yet complete silence when hundreds of men had been killed, and thousands wounded. I saw men who had fought bravely and with great courage denounced as cowards and traitors, and others who had never seen a shot fired hailed as heroes of imaginary victories. And I now know that it is the fashion to say that all recorded history is simply written by the last man with his finger on the typewriter. But I don't believe it. Looking back, I now see that had the West merely put up a few millions in supplying our troops the war might well have been won, because Franco and his gang had all the weapons and we had none. But no-one would listen, and my book was ignored.

Was it all worth it? For me, yes, if only because it opened my eyes to the realities of Fascism, and it made it easier for me a few years later to see the Communist show trials for what they were. So yes, yes, it was all worth it.

Lights down.

Interval.

Scene 8

Barnhill Farmhouse, late spring morning. 1948

McKinnon enters, carrying a covered plate, and a sheaf of papers.

MCKINNON   Yer weekly supply of porridge, Mr. Orwell.

ORWELL   Many thanks. You must remember to thank your wife Morag on my behalf. And tell her that not a grain of sugar has ever dared to alight on its rugged surface. *(He places the plates on the table. Lifts off the top plate and surveys the slabs of porridge.)* You know, I can't for the life of me imagine how I ever ate porridge without the benefit of salt.

MCKINNON   Ye're whit we in the Wee Frees describe as a late conversion, Mr. Orwell, but nane the worse fur that. *(Pause)* Something ah thocht ah should mention, Mr. Orwell — it's getting tae be the talk of the island.

ORWELL   Something I've said, something I've done?

MCKINNON   Naw. It's thae tatties ye gave me last week, the wee ones that ye grew out there in yer garden.

ORWELL   With loving care, with loving care. My Jersey Royals.

MCKINNON   Oh, aye, is that what ye cry them? — Jersey Royals, they're wee, but they're the cat's pyjamas, Mr. Orwell.

ORWELL   Yes, the Royals, the absolute *sine qua non* of the potato world, McKinnon.

MCKINNON   Naebody in Jura has ever tried tae grow them here oan the island, Mr. Orwell.

ORWELL   Correction. It's not Mr. Orwell who grows them, McKinnon.

MCKINNON   Naw?

ORWELL   No, it's Mr. Blair who is your wizard of agriculture, McKinnon, and he is a fellow of a totally different disposition. No, Mr. Orwell, he is the eccentric author, Mr. Blair, he is the gardener.

MCKINNON   Well, please give Mr. Blair ma compliments, but has he telt ye yet how he does it?

ORWELL   Not yet, Blair is very secretive by nature, but when he does, then rest assured that you will be the very first to know. Anything else?

McKinnon moves forward and slowly places the papers on the table. Orwell picks them up and surveys them.

ORWELL   But, but these are comic papers, Mr. McKinnon. These are boys' comic papers.

MCKINNON   Aye, sur, they are that. The *Wizard*, the *Rover*, the *Hotspur* and the *Adventure*.

ORWELL   I see. But... but what on earth leads you to bring them here to me now?

MCKINNON   Yer *Critical Essays*, 1942. Ye wrote an article on Boys' weeklies, Mr. Orwell.

ORWELL   Yes. That caused quite a stir at the time in the Right Wing press, if memory serves me right.

MCKINNON   Did... ye manage tae read all o' these comics, Mr. Orwell?

ORWELL   It was some time back, but yes, most of them. And the others, the *Magnet* and the *Champion*, as I recollect.

MCKINNON   Thae twa' are English comics, Mr. Orwell.

ORWELL   What you really mean is that they don't come from your D.C. Thomson people, over in Dundee.

MCKINNON   Aye.

ORWELL   Can I take it that you do not agree with what I wrote in my essay?

MCKINNON   Well ye mak some guid points, but no' in its entirety — ye see too much in them, sur.

ORWELL   I don't quite catch your drift, McKinnon.

MCKINNON   Ye're saying that these boys' comics like the *Rover* and the *Wizard*, that they're a' political, sur.

ORWELL   You'll have to refresh my memory on what I wrote, McKinnon.

McKinnon slowly withdraws a sheet of paper from his pocket, then puts on his glasses, and peers at the paper.

MCKINNON   "All fiction is censored in the interests of the ruling class... and boys' fiction is sodden with the worst illusions of 1910."

ORWELL   And you don't agree with that?

MCKINNON   No sur, not at all.

ORWELL   Why on earth not?

MCKINNON   Jist you tak' a wee keek at the *Wizard*, sur. That's the wan oan the top.

Orwell slowly opens the comic, and surveys the first page.

ORWELL   Yes, I remember this one — it's a story on athletics called 'Has Wilson Come back?' OK. So it's got a drawing of a barefoot man, dressed in a black Victorian bathing suit, jumping backwards into a high jump sand pit.

Slide of Wilson on the wall.

MCKINNON   Aye. Wilson of the *Wizard*. Naething at a' political aboot the great Wilson, Mr. Orwell.

ORWELL   Certainly not in the long term, because your man Wilson must have broken his back landing in that wretched sandpit.

MCKINNON   Try the *Rover*, sur.

ORWELL   OK, let's have a wee look. Yes. It's a football yarn. Baldy Hogan's the hero, he's the manager.

Slide on wall.

MCKINNON   Aye, he's the one who's got a gypsy goalie who's colour blind.

ORWELL   Ah yes. His team have jerseys with circles on the front, so that goalie knows who to give the ball to. It made good sense.

MCKINNON   And the *Adventure*?

ORWELL   Your classic muscle man — Morgyn the Mighty — he's a sort of poor man's Tarzan, swinging about, righting all manner of wrongs in the jungle.

Slide of Morgyn.

MCKINNON   And here's the detective Sexton Blake—

ORWELL   —he's not much more than a cut-price Sherlock Holmes, I think Blake even lives in Baker Street.

Slide of Sexton Blake.

ORWELL *(shakes his head)* So what's your point then, man?

MCKINNON   That nane o' these tales has anything much tae do wi' politics sur. Wilson of the *Wizard*, he's the greatest athlete in the world — he got the elixir of life frae a hermit back in 1810...

ORWELL   But that must make your man Wilson about a hundred and fifty. A bit old for high jumping, surely.

MCKINNON   Wilson nivver gets any older, sur. Nane o' them do in the comics. But all o' them, Wilson, Sexton Blake, Morgyn the Mighty, even Baldy Hogan, they're no' really grown ups, sur.

ORWELL   What are they, then?

MCKINNON   They're a' wee boys, Mr. Orwell, wee boys. They dinna have any wives or girlfriends, sometimes they dinna even have mithers or faithers.

ORWELL   Then where do they all live?

MCKINNON   These men live, sur, in the minds o' the lads wha' read them.

ORWELL   But these papers — they don't offer boys the world as it really is — they don't ask any questions.

MCKINNON   It's no' the right time fur questions sur, no' at twelve years old. Gie them time. Let those boys dream for a wee while.

ORWELL   So, can I take it that you find no dark political purpose in D. C. Thomson's comic papers?

MCKINNON   Naw, sur. None.

ORWELL   Well, you're perfectly entitled to your opinion, but before you go, might I ask you if you have managed to read any of my other *Critical Essays*?

McKinnon turns round, one hand on the door knob.

MCKINNON   Mr. Orwell, ah've read every single word that ye've ever put on paper, since back in 1931.

Scene 9

Main room, the farmhouse. The door opens and a woman around forty enters, cases in each hand. Orwell is busy typing in the middle of the room as she enters, lays down the cases, and looks round the room.

ORWELL   Avril!

AVRIL   The end of an odyssey, brother dear. Forty-eight hours from London. Now my arrival in Jura, courtesy of the McKinnon Pony Express.

ORWELL   So did Mr. McKinnon bring you up in the car?

AVRIL   No, his wife Morag did the honours.

ORWELL   And where's my boy Richard?

AVRIL   Richard? He's over with the Clan McKinnon.

ORWELL   Until I cease to be toxic to children.

AVRIL   Exactly, no point in taking any chances. So let's just have a good look at you, my big brother Eric.

He stands, hands on hips, in front of her.

ORWELL   Well — do I pass the Avril assessment?

AVRIL   Much better than your Mr Warburg and Mr Connolly predicted. You obviously haven't needed your ration books up here.

ORWELL   Sit down dear, and I'll make you a cup of tea. Kettle's on.

AVRIL   Wonderful. That's going to be my job from now on. What's this?

ORWELL   A Calor gas stove. It's perfectly serviceable.

AVRIL   And the water?

ORWELL   That tap — it's the only one. Cold. But absolutely wonderful water.

She looks at the stove.

AVRIL   And electricity?

ORWELL   As things stand at the moment, the only electricity in Jura lies in my writing. No, electricity, that won't arrive on the island till about 1950.

AVRIL   But that's a lovely log fire over there, Eric.

ORWELL   Yes. This croft probably hasn't really changed much since 1745, I should imagine.

AVRIL   1745?

ORWELL   The Jacobite Rebellion. The last person who stayed here was probably Bonnie Prince Charlie, fleeing from the Redcoats.

AVRIL   Yes, and with that young lady, Flora MacDonald, making his tea.

ORWELL   Amongst other services.

AVRIL   Eric!

He puts the teapot and a mug for her on the table (his is already there). He brings the milk bottle over from the larder. She pours out the tea. Eric sips his.

ORWELL   Marvellous. Strong. You could float a boat on it.

She rises and draws her finger along a shelf.

AVRIL   Your Mr. Warburg, he told me that it would be hot and cold running dust up here, but this... this farmhouse of yours is immaculate, Eric.

ORWELL   All the work of the prodigious Mrs. Morag McKinnon, Avril. An industrious lady indeed.

AVRIL   That's an understatement, Eric — she has seven strapping children.

ORWELL   She's not wee, but she certainly seems to be free with her favours.

AVRIL   She smiles with difficulty, as they say up here. I noticed that right away.

ORWELL   So what do you think?

She explores the place further, reaches and opens a top cupboard. It is full.

AVRIL   It looks as if we can safely forget about ration books, Eric.

ORWELL   Yes, apart from bread — flour — Jura doesn't have that. You know I didn't think that ration books could possibly survive the war.

AVRIL   I seem to remember that you once said that ration books represented some sort of democracy.

ORWELL   Yes Avril, the democracy of food. Pragmatic government — the only way we could possibly win against Hitler. A minimum of 1500 calories a day. It's absolutely amazing how some of the the gaps between rich and poor disappear when you have a war to win.

AVRIL   Needs must when the devil drives.

ORWELL   They eat like kings up here in Jura. Venison. You know, I think that I might well get thoroughly sick of feasting on venison steaks. The sea, the fish — McKinnon says that the local fish speak to me — they actually jump on to my hook. So next week we'll go fishing, out Corryvreckan way.

AVRIL   And what about your precious Water of Life, Eric?

ORWELL   The whisky? Jura Malt, the Nectar of the Gods, Avril.

She reaches across the table and places her hand on his.

AVRIL   Your novel. You haven't really told me yet about what your next novel is all about. First, what's the title?

ORWELL   The title? I've decided to call it *The Last Man in Europe.*

AVRIL   Oh.

ORWELL   You don't like it?

AVRIL   Is it... is it provisional?

ORWELL   Why do I begin to suspect, Avril, that for the first time in your life you are struggling to combine tact with honesty?

AVRIL   No, it's not that, Eric.

ORWELL   Then, what is it then?

AVRIL   I don't know. I can't quite put my finger on it.

ORWELL   Try, Avril. Use them all, if you have to.

AVRIL   Don't be so defensive, Eric.

ORWELL   What else can I possibly be, with over a hundred thousand words that haven't even been put on paper yet? I'm sorry Avril, I really am, but this... this is the point in time when I sometimes begin to get really afraid...

AVRIL   Afraid? You?

ORWELL   Yes. I'm now twenty odd thousand words in, and for all I know, everything that I've written so far may be simply a load of absolute rubbish. And there is nothing ahead of me but another hundred thousand words on this battered old Remington, and a thousand empty sheets of paper, lying there waiting for me on the floor, begging me to fill them.

AVRIL   But surely... surely you've been through all this before.

ORWELL   Yes, of course I have, but no matter how many times I do it, it never really gets any easier. You see, with a novel, I sometimes wonder where on earth it all comes from. It's not like an essay or a review, where you've got a definite subject, lots of facts and ideas that you want to express in a formal way, in order to make a logical, written argument. No, fiction has its own engine, running away somewhere at the back of your mind. It's not like your Vincent Van Gogh — he could sit all day, looking at his bloody sunflowers, they were out there in front of him. But not me, I've got nothing but a blank sheet of paper. Me, I've got bugger all.

AVRIL   Surely you have some idea of where you are going?

ORWELL   Of course I have, but I haven't the slightest idea of how I'm going to get there!

AVRIL   Oh.

ORWELL   But all is not lost. I think I may have got me a good first line. You see you've always got to have a good first line, it's like a hook. You MUST grab the reader's attention. Then you're a made man, then you are on your way.

AVRIL   I see. *(Pause)* So Eric, will you please read me your first line?

ORWELL *(pause)* Here it is, Avril. *(Pause)* Here it is — "It was a bright cold day in April, and the clocks were striking thirteen."

She smiles and nods. Darkness.

Scene 10

Orwell taps away on the typewriter, then stops, rolls a cigarette, and seals it with a lick.

ORWELL   Can I tell you what I've always wanted? I've always wanted to be absolutely irresistible to women. To have them falling all over themselves to get to me, to lust for me, so that I didn't have to go through all that wretched ritual of courting, showing an interest in them. I know that sounds perhaps hard and unfeeling, but I rather think that I'm simply a damaged product of my class, schools like Wellington and Eton, with no girls around to leaven the lump, so to speak. And I am that lump, no looks, permanently coughing and as clumsy as a bull in a china shop. But me, I was lucky, I fell on my feet. I met Eileen O' Shaughnessy, a paragon of a woman. Eileen, she was much too good for someone like me, someone who was only really interested in what is going on in his own head. We had what is now described as an "open" marriage, which is a euphemism for screwing anyone who was remotely willing. But it's rather like having an open mind, all manner of strange things tend to enter it without permission. An open marriage. I'm beginning to think that sex is rather overrated, but then that's perhaps not surprising when I don't even have the breath to finish a cigarette.

He continues typing. Coughs. Darkness.

Scene 11

Night, the small hours. Orwell is head down at his table by his typewriter. Sound of hooves and a horse breathing heavily. It is Boxer.

BOXER   Four legs good, two legs bad.

ORWELL   Boxer, my dear old friend, what in God's name are you doing here?

BOXER   To say sorry for letting you down, Mr. Orwell.

ORWELL   No, Boxer, you didn't let anyone down. It isn't in your nature.

BOXER   If only I had learnt to read, like all of the other animals.

ORWELL   Yes, as I remember it, I only allowed you to get as far as the letter D.

BOXER   It was C, Mr. Orwell.

ORWELL   Yes, not much use in dealing with those wretched pigs. You couldn't ever read their dreadful Seven Commandments.

BOXER   No, not a word, but the hens, they could read, and they clucked me some of them. There was one about no animal sleeping in a bed.

ORWELL   Which the pigs interpreted as sleeping in a bed with sheets. But there was one pig who wouldn't buy that. Would he?

BOXER   Yes, that was Snowball — but Snowball, he was a traitor.

ORWELL.   And a saboteur. That was probably the first time you had ever heard the word "saboteur", Boxer.

BOXER   Yes, it was. I always wondered why none of us ever saw Snowball again.

ORWELL   Because Snowball... Snowball was Trotsky. So that was why he became... a Previous Person.

BOXER   A Previous Person? I don't understand.

ORWELL   No, my dear fellow, of course you don't. You only got as far as the letter C.

BOXER   Would it have made any difference if I had learnt to read?

ORWELL   Well, at least you would have been able to read the words on the side of the van which carted you off to the slaughter house.

BOXER   But it was all so good at the start, Mr. Orwell, all of us farm animals, all working together.

ORWELL   Yes. For the common good, the pigs said.

BOXER   And I was so happy working with all the other animals, even the rats.

ORWELL   So where do you think it all started to go wrong, Boxer?

BOXER   I really think that it all began with the milk — when the pigs said that they needed all of the milk for their mash. Then it was all saboteurs and no food and animals suddenly disappearing.

ORWELL   But Boxer, when they took you away in the van, don't ever forget that all the other animals tried to stop the pigs from doing it.

BOXER   Yes, even the mice made an effort. But that van, it was off and away before anyone could do anything. Yes, off and away, off and away. Goodbye, Mr. Orwell.

Scene 12

Night. Orwell is smoking, a glass of whisky handy, poring over a sheaf of papers — correcting, adding, re-writing completely lost in the task.

Scene 13

Avril is setting the breakfast table as Orwell enters, looks at her.

AVRIL   Your porridge, Eric, salted to perfection.

ORWELL   Forget about the porridge, I'm not interested in the porridge.

AVRIL   Milk, just tell me when to stop.

ORWELL   And I don't give a bugger about the milk. Have you read it? Have you finished it? What do you think?

AVRIL   I think that you should have your porridge, Eric, before it gets cold.

ORWELL   Bugger the porridge, Avril! What do you think of it?

AVRIL   Well, to be honest, I don't really know. I only got as far as page ten.

ORWELL   Page ten!

AVRIL   Because as it stands, it's unreadable, Eric, quite unreadable. Too many crosses-out, too many squiggles, too many alterations. You can't possibly send this to Mr. Warburg, not in this condition, it's an absolute mess.

She gives him the manuscript. He refuses to take it so she puts it on the table. Orwell rises, paces, looks out the window. He's exhausted.

ORWELL   You're certain, Avril?

AVRIL   Yes, utterly, completely certain.

ORWELL *(leafs through the script)* You're right. It's all over the bloody place.

AVRIL   What on earth are you going to do?

ORWELL   Well, I can't possibly send it over to the mainland for typing — they wouldn't make any more sense of it than you did, and the nearest phone is seven miles away.

AVRIL   I might try to do it for you.

ORWELL   You can't type, Avril — just remember your last attempt.

AVRIL   I do. You told me I had done for typing what Quasimodo had done for coat hangers.

ORWELL   I was being generous.

AVRIL   There might be someone in the village—

ORWELL   I doubt if anyone down there, for all their Scottish education has ever even seen a typewriter.

AVRIL   What about Bletchley Park? After all, Alan Turing broke all those German codes.

ORWELL   I'll take that as a desperate attempt to inject a note of levity into the conversation, Avril.

AVRIL   Sorry, dear.

ORWELL *(pause)* I'll type it all again, the whole bloody thing.

AVRIL   ALL of it?

ORWELL   Every single bloody word, Avril. Every single bloody word. Ten thousand words a day, even if it bloody well kills me.

Darkness, and only the sound of endless typing and coughing.

Scene 14

At the door, Winston Smith, holding the manuscript.

WINSTON   I've read it, the whole bloody thing, and I've got a bone to pick with you. You didn't make me a hero, George, and you didn't save me from Big Brother.

ORWELL   In the face of pain, Winston, there are no heroes. After all, they drugged you, they beat you to a pulp, they broke your arm.

WINSTON   I know. I would have said anything, anything simply to get them to stop. Anything.

ORWELL   Then to top it all, I inserted the rats. I knew that would be the clincher, that would finish you off. No-one on earth could have dealt with those wretched rats.

WINSTON   So I betrayed Julia, the woman I loved.

ORWELL   I know. You would have betrayed anyone, you had no option, my friend. I would have done the same.

WINSTON   Yes, after all, I am you and you are me.

ORWELL   Exactly. I really don't know much about anyone else.

WINSTON   So you couldn't make me a hero, like Clark Gable.

ORWELL   I couldn't, Winston, not possibly. It wouldn't have been right, it wouldn't have been a warning.

WINSTON   But who the hell are you trying to warn?

ORWELL   Everyone, Winston, everyone in the whole bloody world.

WINSTON   Everyone. That's a lot, George.

ORWELL   Yes, probably a little too many.

WINSTON   But at the end you had me say 'I love Big Brother'. It's the last line.

ORWELL   Yes, but you didn't, not where it counts, not deep down in your soul. Big Brother couldn't reach you there.

WINSTON   But you're going to write some sort of a sequel, surely you're not going to let Big Brother win?

ORWELL   I think that's all in the balance, Winston, it's up to us. For Big Brother, he's already here among us. Big Brother is here every time a man bites his lip and does nothing when he sees an injustice done. Big Brother is here every time we avoid an Inconvenient Truth, like the USA fighting Hitler, a racist dictator, with segregated regiments. Big Brother is amongst us every moment we allow men to burrow like rats deep below the earth for coal, or enslave women in convents because they have given birth to illegitimate children.

WINSTON   But surely good always triumphs in the end?

ORWELL   We have to hope so, Winston. The problem is how many people end up in gulags or blindfolded and shot against a wall before these gangsters of the future, hell, gangsters of the present, are stopped. But perhaps, perhaps what I and others have written might just manage to keep a few of us awake, prevent some of these thugs getting into power in the first place. But against that, I always remember what my friend, the poet Tommy Eliot, once said to me. Tommy said 'no poem ever written saved a single Jew from Auschwitz.' And he was right.

Scene 15

News on radio. Click as it is turned off. Orwell is exhausted, ill, smoking.

ORWELL   It's done, finished, over. Avril, she wouldn't read it up here, no, she's gone down to the McKinnon croft to read it down there, well away from me. She's been holed up there since morning. *(He turns the radio on again, then clicks it off.)* God in heaven. Just how long does it take to read a couple of hundred bloody pages? *(The croft door opens.)* Avril!

AVRIL *(nods)* Yes, Eric. Yes.

Scene 16

Warburg and Connolly are again drinking at the club. Sound of drinkers at the bar.

CYRIL   Is he finished yet, Fred? Is he finished?

FRED   Yes. I had the final script in front of me this morning. The second draft. It's excellent.

CYRIL   The SECOND draft? But you haven't even got the first one yet!

FRED   Yes and no. I got two drafts, though I don't for the life of me know why Eric sent me the first one, because it's absolute gibberish. Avril got him to type it all again.

CYRIL   That must have taken him ages, Fred. Ages.

FRED   I can't for the life of me work out how he ever managed it. His brain is writing cheques that his body can no longer cash.

CYRIL   We had a saying back at Eton — no-one ever drowned himself in sweat.

FRED   Well, after Corryvreckan, Eric must have come pretty close.

CYRIL   But what he's written — it's publishable?

FRED   Nothing is immediately publishable, you should know that as well as anyone, but I'll soon have our man Astor knock it into shape.

CYRIL   That's good — some more money in the bank account for our Eric. Do you know, a few years back he said to me, "Cyril I've got enough money to last me for the rest of my life, just as long as I die before eight o'clock tomorrow morning."?

FRED   I wish to hell he would show some of that wit in his novels. They're all so bloody bleak. No, this one is thirty thousand copies minimum. He's a made man now. A made man.

CYRIL   But the title — surely it isn't still *The Last Man in Europe*?

FRED   No, Cyril, he's changed it.

CYRIL   To what?

FRED   Brace yourself. *Nineteen eighty-four*. He has called it *Nineteen eighty-four*.

Scene 17

ORWELL   *1984.* Of course, it isn't really *1984,* that was merely the first date that came into my empty head, but I haven't the slightest idea why. It was maybe just 1948 turned around, but rest assured, fifty years from now some potty professor looking for his PhD will be sweating over a twenty-thousand-word thesis on it.

1984. It really has nothing to do with any year in particular, it's now, it's then, everything that I describe in the book, it's all already been done, or at least parts of it. One way or the other, Newspeak, the Thought Police, Doublethink, the Ministry of Truth, something like it has already been done. Hell, I did a bit of Doublethink myself, when I was pumping out propaganda for the BBC a few years ago. But no one has ever taken the trouble to put all these things between the covers of a single book. Except little old me.

What's the message? Simple. Keep your eyes open at all times, don't let the buggers fool you with cod statistics, don't let them engulf you in a wilderness of bureaucrats. Don't let them off by allowing them to answer questions that you didn't ask in the first place, don't let them disappear into massive vanity projects. Because, for God's sake, it isn't rocket science. Someone once said that common sense is so rare that it is frequently mistaken for genius. Then you BE that genius — be a constant pain in the arse to authority. Never let them off the hook. *(Pause)*

But perhaps I am being too naïve. It is always said that in the Kingdom of the Blind, the One-Eyed Man is King. But that's not the way that it usually works out. No, the One-Eyed Man is invariably cast out of the Kingdom, for daring to declare the Heresy of Light. So it's perhaps not surprising that there has never been any great public demand for One-Eyed Men. And I don't think that there ever will be. No. Never. *(Pause)* Ever.

Lights down.

The end.

WHISPER IN THE HEART

CHARACTERS
Mayor Calvados, mayor of Valencia
Orson Welles, film/theatre director, actor, screenwriter
Algernon Carruthers, British television producer
Leni Riefenstahl, dancer, actress, photographer, film director
Mr. Bernstein/Dadda, Welles' mentor
Michael MacLiammoir, Irish actor, theatre director
Adolf Hitler, German dictator 1933-1945
Narrator
Harry Cohn, Hollywood film producer
Greg Toland, Hollywood cameraman
Floyd Odlum, Hollywood film producer
Bud Schulberg, Author, screenwriter
Radio/Carl Phillips, Radio commentator
Officer's voice/Voices

The play can be performed with a cast of 10. Actors can double roles.

Setting
A down-market hotel in Valencia, in the Basque region of Spain. 1955.

Scene 1

There are five chairs at the rear of the stage, three to the left, two to the right. There are three tables in the acting area, the two smaller ones are to the left and right of the acting area (Tables 1 and 3). They each have one chair. A larger table (Table 2) is at the centre. It has two chairs. There is a phone on table 1 and 2. A bottle of water and several glasses on table 2.

A dishevelled bedroom in a tatty Basque hotel. At its centre, a bed in which lies a snoring man... on his face. The telephone rings. The man sits up, a squashed cigar still in his mouth. He sits upright, and hurls the squashed cigar to the floor. The telephone continues to ring. The man traces the wire, and locates the telephone under the blankets.

In another room a man sits at a desk, holding a telephone.

MAN   Am I speaking to Señor Welles?

ORSON *(befuddled)* Yes, this is Orson Welles speaking. But who in God's name are YOU at this time of the morning?

MAN   It is two o'clock in the afternoon, Mr. Welles.

ORSON   Oh. I'll have to take your word for that. Could... could I please have your name, sir?

MAYOR   Calvados.

ORSON *(still confused)* Calvados, that's a brandy. No, you'll have to be something else.

MAYOR   Mayor Calvados, you may remember, Mr. Welles — we were introduced to each other last night, down at the Casino.

ORSON *(still not focussed)* Hold on, Mr. Mayor, hold on...

Orson picks up a cigar from the side-table, and attempts to light it, but the lighter will not work. He picks up a bottle and attempts to pour its contents into a glass. Only a single drip. He nevertheless attempts to drink it, shakes his head, lays it down and props himself up in bed.

ORSON   So what exactly can I do for you, Mr. Mayor?

MAYOR   A very serious charge has been made against you, Mr. Welles.

ORSON   Not those girls? I swear to you, Mr. Calvados, when it was all over, those girls, they knelt down and thanked me on their bended knees. They said it had been an education to them, a lesson for life.

MAYOR   No, Mr. Welles, I know nothing of any girls. No, the charge made against you, it is much more serious than that — it goes back over four hundred years.

ORSON   That's impossible! I'm only forty years old.

MAYOR   Witchcraft, Mr. Welles. Witchcraft.

ORSON   Witchcraft! Who in the Sam Hill is accusing me of witchcraft?

MAYOR   Mr. Correa.

ORSON   And who exactly is he? Valencia's Witchfinder General?

MAYOR   He is the manager of our Casino, and this morning he has pressed formal charges against you with my office.

ORSON   Mr. Calvados, this is not the Dark Ages, and not even Senator Joe McCarthy ever accused me of witchcraft. So, give me a break, I don't have to explain anything, either to you or to your Mr. Correa. OK, so I had a great run of the cards and so I came out a thousand bucks up. So what? What's the big deal?

MAYOR   He claims that you engaged with the spirit world.

ORSON   You mean one knock for yes, two knocks for no?

MAYOR   He is of the opinion that you cast a spell upon his dealer, Mr. Garcia, that you read his mind.

ORSON   Jesus wept. If I could read minds, I would have done it back in Hollywood with Louis B. Mayer and Harry Cohn and I wouldn't be here now with you in this crummy town working for the BBC.

MAYOR   The BBC? You say, Mr. Welles, that you are employed by the British Broadcasting Corporation?

ORSON   Yes. The British Broadcasting Corporation. Commissioned by warrant of Lord Reith himself, and dispatched to you here in Valencia on his behalf with the express responsibility to entertain, edify and instruct the Spanish nation.

MAYOR   Lord Reith, the BBC, that is quite a different matter, Mr. Welles. The English. Fair play.

ORSON   *Tom Brown's Schooldays.*

MAYOR   Mens sana in corpore sano.

ORSON   Yes. The playing fields of Eton, the whole shebang. So, Mr. Calvados, can I take it that we are all clear now?

MAYOR   Yes, I rather think so, Mr. Welles. But if you would please report to me tomorrow morning at the Council offices at your convenience, just to sign some affidavits – a mere formality, I can assure you.

ORSON   Pleased to oblige, Mr. Mayor. And just to finish — let me offer a few words of advice to your friend, Mr. Correa.

MAYOR   Yes?

ORSON   Tell him this — never get into a pissing contest with a skunk.

There is a knocking at the door. Welles gets up and drapes a dressing gown around himself.

ORSON   COME IN!

A formally-dressed, middle-aged man in pinstripes, enters.

CARRUTHERS Good morning, Mr. Welles.

ORSON   Morning, Carruthers . You know, no offence meant, but until I met you, I had never heard of anyone on earth called Carruthers, except maybe a butler in a Noel Coward play.

Carruthers lets it pass.

CARRUTHERS Mr. Welles, those notes you gave me last night for those three young ladies...

ORSON Yes, what about them?

CARRUTHERS They have just informed me that they don't choose to engage in that kind of activity.

ORSON ALL of them?

CARRUTHERS I'm afraid so, sir. There appeared to be a general consensus of opinion amongst the ladies on the matter.

ORSON Very odd. Standard practice down in Rio. Ten bucks apiece. I've done it down there loads of times.

CARRUTHERS Perhaps, sir, but not here in Spain.

ORSON Those ladies — did they ask you to explain it all to them — in Spanish?

CARRUTHERS Yes, but I must confess I'm not at all certain that I could have done so, even in English.

ORSON But come on, Carruthers. You told me that you had been to Eton.

CARRUTHERS Harrow.

ORSON Same thing. So you're telling me that you gave it your best shot, but that it was no dice.

CARRUTHERS As you say sir, no dice.

ORSON Well, perhaps, perhaps it might have lost a little in the translation. Maybe I should sketch it all out for those little ladies on a sheet of paper.

CARRUTHERS Yes, sir. I am sure that some diagrams might well prove to be of great value. But I would suggest, with the greatest respect, several sheets of paper. Perhaps a manual might be best.

ORSON But you did manage to secure my... medication?

NARRATOR Carruthers lifts a bottle out of a paper bag, and hands it to Orson, who studies the label.

CARRUTHERS Glenmorangie, full malt, sir. Twenty years old.

ORSON   Nectar, nectar. Nothing on earth like it, Carruthers. *(He pours himself a shot.)* Fancy a shot?

CARRUTHERS Much too early for me, I'm afraid, sir. *(He looks at his watch)* When do you want to meet the crew tomorrow? After breakfast?

ORSON   Carruthers, this IS breakfast. *(He takes a big slug, and sighs)* You know, we've known each other for nearly a month — you are my producer — I really can't keep calling you Carruthers, it's not very good for my sanity, so what's your first name, man?

CARRUTHERS Algernon, sir.

ORSON   Then it's probably best that we stay where we are, at least for the moment. Our consultant, when does she get here?

CARRUTHERS She arrived at reception just a few moments ago. She will be in her room.

ORSON   Oh. Then we sure as hell better start to clean up in here. Or at least try to rearrange the dust.

Carruthers uneasily starts to brush the floor and picks up a used condom. He reaches into an inside pocket for an envelope, into which he delicately inserts the offending condom, goes to lick the envelope, but decides against it. He looks around, finally locates a dustbin in a corner and gently drops the envelope into it.

ORSON   Our consultant — did she set any ground rules?

CARRUTHERS   Only two that she has so far brought to my direct attention. Number one is no first names, at least not for the moment.

ORSON   And the second?

CARRUTHERS No... no unnecessary physical contact.

ORSON   Oh. Very formal. Very English.

CARRUTHERS Hardly, sir, under the circumstances.

The telephone rings. Orson answers it.

ORSON   Tell the lady to come right on up.

CARRUTHERS Do you wish me to bring up a script?

ORSON   Yes, the final version that I gave you yesterday. We'll need that.

Carruthers leaves. Orson straightens his tie, draws a hand through his hair, and picks up a script from the table and scrutinises it. There is a knock on the door.

ORSON   Come in.

NARRATOR   The door opens and a slim, athletic middle-aged lady enters.

LENI   Good afternoon, Mr. Welles.

Orson walks across to kiss her hand. She recoils slightly.

ORSON   Glad you could make it, Miss Riefenstahl.

Scene 2

Orson and Leni sit at a table sipping wine. Leni is surveying a script. She lays it down.

LENI   So what exactly do you require of me, Mr. Welles? What are to be my precise terms of reference?

ORSON   Very simple, Miss Riefenstahl. Two things. The BBC have commissioned a series of travelogues called *Round the World With Orson Welles*. This one, on the Basques, it's the third of the series.

LENI   I see. And where exactly would I fit in?

ORSON   Jai Lai.

LENI   Jai Lai? I do not understand.

ORSON   The game. You may know it better as Pelota, Miss Riefenstahl.

LENI   Yes, I remember. A wall game.

ORSON   Not just a wall game, Miss Riefenstahl, THE wall game. For the Basques, Pelota is a matter of life and death, it's what they ARE — they've got more versions of it than the positions in the *Kama Sutra*.

LENI   You have a quaint turn of phrase, Mr. Welles.

ORSON   A family trait, ma'am.

LENI   And my role?

ORSON   To be my eyes, and to help me with the editing. Because, I've seen your *Olympia* — I know every single frame of that movie — hell, I'm on speaking terms with some of the guys in the crowd. You've got an eye for the physical, ma'am.

LENI   And will I be contracted by Lord Reith?

ORSON   No. I don't work for Lord Reith.

LENI   But... you told me that you did.

ORSON   Lord Reith, he was put out to pasture by the BBC way back in 1938.

LENI   But I understood...

ORSON   I lied, I lied in my teeth. Got you here, didn't it?

LENI   Yes. It did.

ORSON   Which was the sole purpose of the exercise.

LENI   And the BBC, will they provide me with a formal contract?

ORSON   No, they won't. Your contract will be with me.

LENI   Was it too soon for the English?

ORSON   Much too soon. Those English, they wouldn't touch you with a bargepole, ma'am. No, they pay me and I pay you. Simple.

LENI   That is very generous.

ORSON   No, for I can assure you that you will sweat for every dollar you earn. Anyhow, money isn't where it's at; it never is, not for people like you and me.

LENI   You are right. I don't have any money.

ORSON   But you are not poor.

LENI   No. I am not poor. *(Pause)* I believe you mentioned TWO things, Mr. Welles.

ORSON   Yes, and this is where I'm somewhat in the dark. Carruthers has got some other project for you, and I don't know anything about it.

LENI   The same terms?

ORSON   I thought you told me that you weren't interested in money?

LENI   I need it to buy a watch. I was late for our meeting, Mr.Welles. I have no watch.

ORSON   Of course you have.

LENI   Sorry?

ORSON   Check inside your handbag, Miss Riefenstahl.

Leni fumbles in her handbag and withdraws a watch.

LENI   Where on earth has this come from?

ORSON   Let's just say it arrived in Valencia by courtesy of Lord Reith.

LENI *(examines it)* This is a Cartier, Mr. Welles.

ORSON   No, ma'am, it's a fake, but I've been assured that it might just occasionally tell the time. *(He takes it from her and attaches it to her wrist)* There you are.

She flinches as he touches her, then she examines it.

LENI   Wonderful. So if you don't mind, I will make my way down to the Pelota courts, and I will see you back here in the hotel for dinner. *(She stands)*

ORSON   Will you play?

LENI   Of course I will play. There is no other way to learn.

ORSON   They say that Pelota can be a pretty demanding game, Miss Riefenstahl. I don't want to seem ungentlemanly, but...

LENI   Age has nothing to do with it, Mr. Welles. Have you ever been seriously involved in sport?

ORSON   Only once.

LENI   And which sport would that be?

ORSON   Bullfighting.

LENI   Oh. Well, tomorrow you can observe a woman of fifty-five play pelota, and later I will come over to the Plaza, and watch you fight a bull.

ORSON   I think you may just have got yourself a deal, Miss Riefenstahl.

Scene 3

The following day. Bullfighting music. Orson, sweating and bloodied, supported by Carruthers, and dressed in a tattered bullfighter's costume, staggers into the room. He sits wearily down at the table.

ORSON *(groaning)* Glenmorangie, Carruthers. *(Carruthers pours him out a shot, which Orson gulps down)* No, a bird can't fly on one wing. Let's have another look at that bottle, man. *(He pours himself another shot and gulps it down.)*

CARRUTHERS Are you sure that this is entirely wise, Mr. Welles?

ORSON   Wise? What has wise got to do with it? *(He pours himself another glass)* Round the teeth and over the gums, watch out stomach, here it comes. *(He gulps it down, and pours another. There is a knock at the door.)*

CARRUTHERS That will be Miss Riefenstahl. Should... might it be best that I ask her to come back later?

ORSON   No, open the door, let her in, man. Let her see me warts and all.

Carruthers opens the door, to reveal Leni.

LENI   Very impressive. You surprise me, Mr. Welles.

ORSON   A pity I didn't surprise the bull.

CARRUTHERS They did offer to let you practice first with that strange contraption on wheels, sir.

ORSON   The trolley? That's for amateurs. I'm well beyond that, Carruthers.

LENI   When did you last fight a bull, Mr. Welles?

ORSON   Not long ago.

LENI   How long ago?

ORSON   When I first came to Spain, as a boy.

LENI   But not in the arena itself?

ORSON   No, never — sometimes they used to let me work out with some of the young bulls, just like today.

CARRUTHERS Would you like anything to drink, Ma'am?

LENI   Just some iced water for me, Mr. Carruthers.

Carruthers leaves.

LENI   You are very brave, Mr. Welles.

ORSON   No, Miss Riefenstahl. Just very vain. *(He takes a slug.)* I was just showing off to a lady, and that... that is always dangerous. Unless you can manage to do it right. And I didn't.

LENI   Then perhaps this is the wrong time.

ORSON   For what?

LENI   For us to talk about our project. I spent most of yesterday looking at Pelota, then playing it.

ORSON   And playing it very well, from what Carruthers tells me.

LENI   Those young Basques were carrying me, Mr. Welles, I know that. But as you said, Pelota is really lots of quite different games.

ORSON   Yes, all tailored to different needs, different ages.

LENI   Exactly.

ORSON   And like all sports, essentially pointless.

LENI   Fantasy.

ORSON   Like baseball in the States.

LENI   Yes, but, here… it is a sort of statement of what it is to be a Basque. I have done some research. No one knows where the Basques came from. They arrived in Spain from nowhere about a thousand odd years ago.

ORSON   A mystery to themselves.

LENI   So somehow you — we — have to get that down on film.

ORSON   With Carruthers, and a cameraman who doesn't even speak English.

LENI   But he is a Scotchman.

ORSON   That's exactly what I mean, Miss Riefenstahl.

Scene 4

Orson's hotel room. A day later. Carruthers is tidying up the room as Leni enters.

LENI   Who are all those people standing out in the street, Mr. Carruthers?

CARRUTHERS They are waiting for Mr. Welles, ma'am.

LENI   To what purpose?

CARRUTHERS I believe that he owes them money.

LENI   ALL of them?

CARRUTHERS I am afraid so, Miss Riefenstahl.

LENI   What for?

CARRUTHERS Mostly hotels and food, ma'am. Not for himself, you understand, but for his actors. Mr. Welles seems to have something of a soft spot for actors. He always puts them up in the very best hotels, champagne and caviar, all that sort of thing. Mr. Welles is a very generous man, especially with other people's money.

LENI   Why doesn't he just go out there and pay them?

CARRUTHERS Because Mr. Welles lives a champagne lifestyle on a lemonade income, ma'am.

LENI   But these men out there, they seem to have come here from all over Europe.

CARRUTHERS Yes. Mr. Welles is exceptionally versatile. He is generous with other people's money in a whole range of different currencies.

LENI   Rather like his Harry Lime character in that film, *The Third Man.*

CARRUTHERS Exactly. Mr. Welles always has twenty balls in the air at the same time.

Orson sweeps in.

ORSON   And two of those balls are always my OWN!

CARRUTHERS Did these gentlemen out there try to stop you, Mr. Welles ?

ORSON   No, not a chance. I sneaked in by the back door, but I found one of them waiting there for me, at the bottom of the stairs so we cut cards for what I owed him. Double or quits. He lost.

CARRUTHERS I will go out and try to take care of them. Will I inform them that their cheques are in the post?

ORSON   Yes. From London, from the BBC, from Lord Reith. That always seems to go down well.

CARRUTHERS But Lord Reith left the BBC in 1938, Mr. Welles.

ORSON   Who gives a damn? Some hick from Milan isn't going to know that, man.

CARRUTHERS Indeed.

He leaves. Leni shakes her head in disbelief.

LENI   I would like you to have a look at this — I edited it last night. *(They sit at a table, at the editor, and peer at it.)* This is your sequence with the two old priests, playing pelota against the church wall.

Orson moves to survey it.

ORSON   To film is heaven, to edit divine, Miss Riefenstahl.

LENI   Exactly.

Orson checks the film.

ORSON   Perfect, Miss Riefenstahl. Couldn't have done it better myself.

LENI   Yes, of course you could. I have seen some of your work. You know how to find the moment.

ORSON   Yes, finding the moment, that is what movies are all about. *(He picks up a bottle and pours out a glass.)* Care for a shot?

LENI   No, thank you.

Orson gulps it down.

ORSON   Miss Riefenstahl, I have a little confession to make to you.

LENI   Then confess.

ORSON   I didn't invite you over here to Valencia simply for the pelota. Or out of pity.

LENI   I didn't really think that you had.

ORSON   No?

LENI   My Scotch friend, John Grierson, he told me that he had spoken to you last month in London. He said that you felt sorry for me.

ORSON   No. Sympathy, not pity.

LENI   Do you think that I have been hard done by?

ORSON   Hard done by, that's very Scotch. No, let's just say that I would like to get to know you.

LENI   But that means questions. I have spent the last ten years since the war answering questions, Mr. Welles.

ORSON   Perhaps not the same questions that I may wish to ask, ma'am.

LENI   Yes, but only on two conditions. If you are going to ask me questions, then you must provide me with exactly the same opportunity.

ORSON   And second?

LENI   That you must always tell me the truth.

ORSON   And if the truth turns out to be impossible, then you'll just have to sit back and enjoy the lies.

LENI   Simply tell me what happened. The facts.

ORSON   The facts are not always the truth.

LENI   Let's call it a journey of self-discovery. Which always starts with a single step.

ORSON   So does falling down stairs. *(Pause)* So this exercise may prove to be somewhat dangerous, Miss Riefenstahl.

LENI   For both of us.

ORSON   Perhaps, but before we get going, please promise me just one thing.

LENI   Yes.

ORSON   That what is said here stays here.

LENI   Who on earth could I possibly tell?

ORSON   You're right. You probably have more to lose than me.

LENI   No. I have lost everything already, Mr. Welles. But your life is still ahead of you.

ORSON   Tell that to those guys back in Hollywood, tell it to those hyenas hovering in the Plaza.

LENI   Hyenas do not hover, Mr. Welles.

ORSON   You know what I mean. But OK, do you want to make a start?

LENI   At first, I was a dancer.

A slide/movie of her as a dancer appears.

ORSON   Ballet?

LENI   No, it was what you might call free dance, rather like Isadora Duncan. I played to full houses all over Germany, back in the 1920s.

ORSON   And then there was silent film?

LENI   Yes. The mountain movies of Arnold Fanck.

We see slide/film of a Fanck movie.

LENI   So pure, the mountains, all snow and ice. Fanck, he was a genius.

Fanck appears at table 1.

LENI   He found me.

FANCK   Found me? Leni Riefenstahl hunted me down like an animal! She was voracious, remorseless. She couldn't climb, she couldn't ski, she couldn't do anything that I needed her to do. OK, I admit she looked absolutely marvellous, but that wasn't going to make a blind bit of difference, climbing barefoot up a cliff.

LENI   Of course, I had never skied, I had certainly never climbed. But I had learnt to jump, I had learnt to throw, I had learnt to dance. Fanck just had to give me a chance, and I knew that I wouldn't let him down.

FANCK   She didn't let me down, no never once, no, not for a single moment. Yes, she sprained her ankles, she broke her leg, but Leni never gave up. So, soon she was climbing barefoot up some of the most difficult climbs in the Alps, and sometimes even without ropes. She gave me great shapes, great images. Leni gave herself completely to me in every film that I made.

Slide/film of Leni climbing barefoot.

LENI   Fanck. He was absolutely marvellous.

ORSON   Your mentor.

FANCK   And Leni, she was a very grateful young woman. OK, so she also slept with her ski instructors, but that didn't really bother me. No, a little of Leni, that was quite enough for a man of my age.

LENI   It wasn't the acting, it wasn't the climbing, no it was watching Fanck editing, that was an education for me, how he told the story through film. He was a master, a master of his craft.

Scene 5

Carruthers' room, the following day. Carruthers enters, carrying a reel of film.

CARRUTHERS I have seen what you have done with the first part of the film that I brought here from London for you, Miss Riefenstahl. Wonderful.

LENI   It was very difficult, even with the script that you gave me. Lots of film, but no clear order. But I cut the first reel down to five minutes, and I think it makes sense now. I do hope so. However did you manage to get hold of it?

CARRUTHERS Old Boys' Network. They call it the Hollywood Raj, a little group of English actors and directors out there in California. Lord Reith's chums found it somewhere in the studio rubbish, and sent it over to him in London.

LENI   Rubbish? It's a glorious piece of cinema. Glorious.

CARRUTHERS What ultimately appeared on the screen twelve years ago bears no resemblance to what Mr. Welles first conceived. They – the studio – they butchered it.

LENI   But the rest of this ending you have given me, surely it must be out there somewhere.

CARRUTHERS Probably, mouldering away on some studio shelf. But those awful Hollywood people, they will never let Mr. Welles touch it. Never.

LENI   How awful. But who is paying me for this work?

CARRUTHERS Lord Reith. You see, I rather think that for him, Mr.Welles represents everything that he could never hope to be himself. Creative, articulate, outrageous...

LENI   Promiscuous.

CARRUTHERS That too. *(Pause)* You see, Lord Reith very much admires those who unlike him, have pushed the boundaries, so to speak. And who have a feeling of self-worth.

LENI   Like Orson Welles. He likes himself, doesn't he?

CARRUTHERS No – he likes you. He loves himself.

LENI   So it was Lord Reith who got me here to Valencia.

CARRUTHERS Yes, Miss Riefenstahl. He gave me the additional funds to bring someone out here to help Mr. Welles. But don't ever tell him, please.

LENI   But why did you choose me?

CARRUTHERS Miss Riefenstahl. Let me first tell you a little story, something personal, something very important to me. Do you have the time?

LENI   Of course.

CARRUTHERS *(gathers himself)* I first met Horst Harbig at Harrow in 1920. I was only twelve, but I thought he was the most beautiful thing that I had ever seen. *(Pause)* And in that moment I knew who I was, and who I would always be.

LENI Were there many Germans at Harrow back in those days?

CARRUTHERS No, not many, and certainly none like Horst; no one remotely like him.

LENI But... but surely there are always schoolboy crushes at all-boy schools?

CARRUTHERS Yes, but even then, that first day, I knew that this was much more than that, more than a crush. I knew, right from the start exactly what I was, at the centre of my being. Goodness, I hated sport but I even tried out for the school rugby team. And I loathed rugby.

LENI Because Horst was a rugby player.

CARRUTHERS Yes, he was a winger. Horst could run like the wind. Those legs...

LENI Yes, legs.

CARRUTHERS Long, slim, muscular...

LENI Yes, legs.

CARRUTHERS Yes, as you said, there were lots of schoolboy crushes at Harrow in those days, usually young boys on the older lads, the prefects.

LENI Punctuated by regular beatings, or so I've been told.

CARRUTHERS Yes. The English disease – I believe they used to call it, over in Europe. But Horst and I, we were the same age. And we only laid hands on each other once.

LENI Once?

CARRUTHERS Yes. It was Saturday, September 4th, 1920. The House rugby trials. I only played because of Horst...

LENI Contact.

CARRUTHERS Yes, contact. I can see it all even now, in my mind's eye. Horst was going hard for the line, an absolutely certain try, and I was defending, at full back, the last line of defence. I drove into him hard at the top of his thighs, both arms firm around him, head down, and I put him straight into touch. A perfect tackle, the first tackle of my life... and the last. And it was wonderful, wonderful.

LENI   Yes, like some glorious, marvellous leap, when you suddenly clear a height you have never before achieved.

CARRUTHERS Yes. It was as if, for a brief moment, I had engulfed Horst, absorbed him.

LENI   Yes.

CARRUTHERS And Horst, he stood up and he smiled and shook me by the hand. And the two of us were firm friends from that moment on.

LENI   But never...

CARRUTHERS No, no, never. Horst, he went back to Germany five years later and he became a doctor, then a surgeon, but we never for a moment lost touch.

LENI   Mr. Carruthers, I do not wish to be rude, but why are you telling me all this?

Carruthers slowly withdraws a pistol, and lays it on the table.

CARRUTHERS Because, Miss Riefenstahl, I brought you to Spain in order to kill you. *(Pause)* Don't worry, I'm not certain I even know how to fire the wretched thing.

LENI   But why?

CARRUTHERS Let me try to tell you. Horst and I stayed close — he would come over to stay with me every summer, or I would travel over to see him in Berlin. Then in 1934, he became a surgeon and married, and he brought his wife, Helga with him to stay with me in England. It was marvellous. 1934 that was the year when you made your film *Triumph of the Will.*

LENI   Yes. My fall from grace.

CARRUTHERS We saw your film that next year, in Berlin. We all thought that it was absolutely wonderful. Then.

LENI   Yes, yes. It won prizes all over Europe.

CARRUTHERS Then in 1936, the Party told Horst that he must divorce Helga.

LENI   Because Helga was Jewish?

CARRUTHERS Yes. But Horst refused to divorce her.

LENI   As many Germans did.

CARRUTHERS Then, in 1938, he was commissioned to perform an operation on your Führer.

LENI   Yes, I remember. I didn't know it was him. A polyp in the throat. But Horst was married to a Jew.

CARRUTHERS From all accounts, it was Adolf Hitler who decided who was a Jew and who was not.

LENI   Yes. That sounds about right.

CARRUTHERS Horst did an excellent job. So they were safe, at least for the moment. At least until 1940.

LENI   1940.

CARRUTHERS The RAF bombed Berlin and Horst was injured in the raid... his hands. He could never operate again.

LENI   Stop, stop! I don't think that I want to hear any more.

CARRUTHERS Miss Riefenstahl. I'm afraid you must. In September 1941, Helga was dispatched to Auschwitz, and Horst insisted on going with her. They were never seen again.

LENI   Please, please don't tell me any more.

CARRUTHERS Not much more to tell, Miss Riefenstahl. Only one thing. Back in July 1941, Horst had left me a message at the American Embassy — he had an old Harrow friend at their office. Old Boys' Club again. *(Pause)* I still have that letter, it goes everywhere with me. Horst, I think he knew what was coming and he felt that he had to write it. *(Pause)* He said that he loved me, that he had experienced the very same feelings as I had, all those long years ago. All those wasted years.

LENI   If he had come to England to be with you...

CARRUTHERS Then he need never have died. But Helga would have perished. Nothing could possibly have saved her. *(Pause)* So your Führer killed the only person whom I ever truly loved.

LENI   The Führer knew nothing of this.

CARRUTHERS No, not the detail. But when a fish stinks, Miss Riefenstahl, it stinks from the head. Hitler killed Horst Harbig, he didn't have to put it in writing. Himmler, Eichmann, all that rotten gang, they knew exactly what their Führer wanted them to do.

LENI   But I had nothing to do with it, Mr. Carruthers. I've been through this dozens of times.

CARRUTHERS But Hitler, he was your friend. He listened to you.

LENI   Yes, he did, but that was only when we discussed art, film, literature, but the moment we got on to politics, he became the Führer, and became an altogether different person. And me, I had to mind my place, so I held my tongue. If that makes me an evil person, then shoot me now...

CARRUTHERS *(puts away the gun)* No. Killing you would have been an indulgence, a sort of revenge for Horst, but in the end essentially pointless. *(Pause)* Anyhow, I have seen you with the children, I have seen you with the priests, I have seen you with Mr. Welles. And I flatter myself that I am a good judge of character.

LENI   Thank you.

CARRUTHERS And others, others better placed than you, they tried to stop him.

LENI   Yes, I remember. The Von Stauffenberg assassination plot.

CARRUTHERS But life is strange. If only a briefcase had not been moved, a couple of feet, millions of lives could well have been saved. If there were a God, surely he would have moved that briefcase back. Or made sure that Hitler had never been born in the first place.

LENI   Me, I often think back upon those days. And I think to myself — what could I have done?

CARRUTHERS Best if you had simply been incompetent, Miss Riefenstahl. Best that you made an absolutely awful film back in 1934 instead of your wonderful, terrible *Triumph of the Will*. Life would have been so much better for you.

LENI   Yes, you are right. It certainly would.

Scene 6

Orson's room. Next day. Leni and Orson sit drinking coffee at a table.

LENI   My turn now, I think, Mr. Welles.

ORSON   Do we REALLY have to go through with all this?

LENI   Yes, I think so, Mr. Welles. Do you pray?

ORSON   No. I don't want to bore God.

LENI   But you do believe in him?

ORSON   I'll take the Fifth Amendment on that.

LENI   Well, I don't, not after all that I have been through, I really can't. But what I DO believe in is Forces.

ORSON   Forces.

LENI   Yes, energies. A sort of spirit...

ORSON   The spirit that blows where it wills.

LENI   Yes. A Force, an energy that drives people, artists like us onwards, always onwards. And now for some reason, I think, because of that force, the two of us are threaded into this moment.

ORSON   That's a sudden change of metaphor, Miss Riefenstahl. Forces don't usually thread themselves into anything.

They usually blow it away.

LENI   But you must surely know what I mean.

ORSON   Yes, of course I do. But one rule from here on, if we two are going to be doing all this threading together. So let's make it Leni and Orson from now on. All this precious German formality, it's beginning to wear me out.

LENI   Good. Leni and Orson it is, from this moment on. Agreed.

ORSON   So it's me now, I suppose, it's my turn. So precisely where would you like me to start?

LENI   At the very beginning — when you were a child.

ORSON   OK, so let's get started. I was a very old child.

LENI   How old?

ORSON   Ancient.

LENI   That's pretty old.

ORSON   And right from the very start I realised that I was quite remarkable.

LENI   How did you know that?

ORSON   Because Mr. Bernstein told me. Dadda told me.

Bernstein appears and crosses to table 3.

BERNSTEIN   Orson always called me Dadda, Dadda — I just Ioved that... yes, I knew for certain my little Orson was a genius, right from the git-go, it was as plain as the nose on your face that my boy was destined for great things.

ORSON   Yes, Dadda, he told me that when I was eighteen months old, I stood up in my cot and I said "The practice of medicine is what separates us from the animals."

LENI   You said that at the age of eighteen months?

ORSON   Probably a slight exaggeration, Leni. I must have been at least three at the time.

LENI   This man, Mr. Bernstein, Dadda — how did you first come to meet him?

ORSON   He was a friend of my mother.

DADDA   Me, I was head over heels in love with his mother Beatrice, a beautiful woman, a true goddess. Back then, I worshipped the very ground that lady walked on. But hey, don't you get the wrong idea — this was romantic love, the balcony, not the bedroom. Never in my life did I lay a hand upon the fair Beatrice. There's a great deal to be said for romantic love. No guilt and not nearly as messy.

LENI   And where exactly did your father place in all of this?

ORSON   My father was an inventor, a very modest man. Quiet.

DADDA   His father was a hopeless lush, always two drinks away from his brains. Completely unsuitable to bring up a brilliant boy like my Orson, and I reckoned that it was all going to be up to me. So, by the tender age of five, Orson had read the complete works of Shakespeare, but me, I thought — don't ask me why — that his best chance of success might well be in music.

ORSON   My first experience in the arts was in music, and I was pretty dam' good, even if I say so myself.

LENI   As you would.

ORSON   And when my family moved off to Chicago, Dadda followed us there. Dadda, he had lots of good contacts in music in the Windy City, so soon he had me conducting the Chicago Philharmonic Orchestra. So me, I stood in front of these old pros with my tiny baton, waving my little arms about like a windmill. And those good ole boys in the Philharmonic, they just grinned and got on doing pretty much what they would have done anyway.

LENI   But what age were you then?

ORSON   Oh, by that time well into middle age. I think I was around six.

LENI   And what next?

ORSON   I was a rabbit.

LENI   Sorry?

ORSON   I was a rabbit in Marshal Fields department store, and I was one helluva rabbit, I can tell you. And the tips, the tips they came a-pouring in. Good money. Big bucks. *(Pause)* Then, a year later, my parents, they got divorced.

LENI   And how did that affect you?

ORSON   Not very much, if truth be told. Because every time that I stayed with one of them I got twice the love. *(Pause)* But then, when I was nine, my mom died. That... that was a different ball game. Her going, that hit me real hard.

LENI   What about your friend, Dadda?

ORSON   Oh, he got me a part in an opera — *Samson and Delilah* — and that was when I lost my virginity.

LENI   At the age of nine?

ORSON   Yes. It was to one of the chorus girls, a Philistine, Doris, I think her name was. I rather think that curiosity got the better of Doris. Funny how you can lose something that you didn't know you possessed.

LENI   And did you... did you like it?

ORSON   Yes, I found that I liked sex from the very start. Of course at the beginning I wasn't quite certain where everything was put, but once I sorted out the anatomy, we did it for the run of the play. Awake, Orson, the Philistine is upon you! Doris, she was upon me three or four times a week. *(Pause)* But hold on, I think it's your turn now, Leni.

LENI   As you wish.

ORSON   So, when did you first meet him?

LENI   Who?

ORSON   You know who.

The sound of Hitler, raging, in a speech.

LENI   It was in 1933, at the SportPalast. *(Hitler again)* I was stunned. It was, it was as if the earth's hemisphere has suddenly opened up... and split down the middle. *(Hitler again)* Spouting an immense jet of water, that touched the sky and shook the earth.

ORSON   You were banjaxed.

LENI   Banjaxed ?

ORSON   A phrase that I picked up in auld Ireland, when I was just a boy.

LENI   When did you go to Ireland?

ORSON   When I was sixteen, Dadda had sent me off to Europe, with a couple of hundred bucks, and I ended up broke wandering around Ireland in a donkey cart.

LENI   What about your education?

ORSON   Dadda always told me that you should never let your education interfere with your studies.

LENI   Your Dadda, he seems to have been a very wise man.

ORSON   So when I ran out of money travelling around Ireland, I turned up at the Gate Theatre in Dublin and got me an interview with their director, Mike McLiammoir.

Michael MacLiammoir appears.

MICHAEL   Orson Welles — a lying young bastard, if ever I saw one — he told me he had just come over from playing King Lear on Broadway. He hadn't two pennies to rub together, just a moth-eaten old mule and a hole in the seat of his pants. But God help me, from the start there was something about that boy... I'm struggling to find the word, it's Jewish. *(Pause)* Chutzpah, that's the word, chutzpah. Orson had enough of that for all of us at the Gate, bejasus he had enough for the whole of bloody Ireland. So me, I get our boyo some lodgings, hot and cold running dust, a couple of quid a week and cakes, and before you can say Jack Johnson, Orson is up there playing Chekhov and Shakespeare. And he was the best Mark Antony that I ever did see.

ORSON   'When that the poor have cried, Caesar has wept,

Ambition should be made of sterner stuff,

Yet Brutus says he was ambitious

And Brutus is an honourable man

You all did see that on the Lupercal

I thrice presented him a kingly crown

Which twice he did refuse — was this ambition?'

LENI *(claps)*   Bravo!

ORSON   Hold on! You're a clever one, Leni, you stopped, just when it was getting to be interesting. We were in the Sportpalast, 1933. And, if memory serves me right, you were busy exploding.

LENI   You are laughing at me, Orson.

ORSON   No, I'm not. Keep going, Leni, keep going.

LENI   I was stunned, paralysed... and I decided that I just had to meet this man, Hitler.

ORSON   So you wrote to him?

LENI   Of course. And a week later I was picked up at the station at Wilhelmshaven and taken in a big Rolls Royce to the Imperial Hotel. We met on the beach.

Scene 7

Sound of seagulls.

HITLER   Miss Riefenstahl, this letter of yours, it is really quite a remarkable coincidence, because I had already told my man Captain Bruckner that I wished to make your acquaintance. Your dance by the sea in *The Holy Mountain,* it moved me very deeply.

LENI   Thank you.

HITLER   When I come to power, you must make my films for me.

LENI   Herr Hitler, I have just refused a commission from the Catholic church. I can't possibly work to order, that's not really what my art is about.

IIITLER   I can now begin to understand your predicament, Miss Riefenstahl. You see, in other times, I was something of an artist myself. Perhaps, perhaps when you are a little older you may find it possible to embrace some of my ideas, and to express them in your films.

LENI   Perhaps...

ORSON   And that was it?

LENI   Not quite.

ORSON   He didn't make a pass at you?

LENI   No, well not exactly. The Führer, he was magnetic, but no, not in a sexual way.

ORSON   Like opera without the music.

LENI   But let's return to Ireland.

ORSON   Well, I had me a great time in Dublin. Hell, I played everything from Macbeth to de Maupassant. It's really amazing what you can do when you don't give a damn. Then it was back to New York and hot and cold running dust again. I think that we're about in line now, Leni, give or take a couple of years.

LENI   I'm in 1934.

Scene 8

Leni and Hitler.

HITLER   Your budget for our Nuremberg Rally film, Miss Riefenstahl...

LENI   Yes, Führer?

HITLER   The cameras, Miss Riefenstahl, I had no idea that the Reich could possibly possess so many cameras. Four times as many as you used in last year's Rally.

LENI   Five, Führer.

HITLER   But your film last year, it was an excellent record of the Rally. Everyone in the Party said so.

LENI   But this will not, under any circumstances, be an excellent record, Führer.

HITLER   No? Explain.

LENI   This year's film will not provide merely an account of what occurs, Führer. *(Pause)* No, it will be much more than that, it will be a vision, a dream.

HITLER   My dream.

LENI   Yes, Führer, your dream. This time, this time we will frame the Rally round the film, not the other way round. Thus, every moment, everything that happens in Nuremberg, will revolve round my cameras. A vast, shifting kaleidoscope of power, of strength, of beauty – a hymn to Germany, to the Third Reich.

HITLER   To our volk, our people.

LENI   And to you, Führer, to you.

HITLER   So not a mere record. Not the truth.

LENI   Yes, Führer, the truth, but YOUR truth.

HITLER   And do you have any title in mind?

LENI   No, Führer, not yet. But it must reflect our right, our destiny, our will, and how, despite all the darkness of the years since the war, Germany will inevitably triumph.

HITLER   Yes. A triumph of the will.

Sequence from Triumph of the Will.

ORSON   A great movie.

LENI   But the worst thing that I could possibly have created.

ORSON   Your albatross.

LENI   Around my neck, for the rest of my life... But back to you.

ORSON   Tomorrow, Leni, tomorrow. My memory, I think it's beginning to go into deep spasm. Let's start again tomorrow.

Scene 9

NARRATOR   A day later. Carruthers' room. Mayor Calvados enters.

Carruthers shakes his hand, and beckons him sit to down.

CARRUTHERS   A pleasure to see you again, Mr. Calvados. Please sit yourself down right there.

CALVADOS   Thank you very much, Mr. Carruthers.

CARRUTHERS   You'll join me in a Glenmorangie?

CALVADOS   Thank you, but it is a little too early for me, Mr. Carruthers.

CARRUTHERS   Mr. Welles tells me that it is never too early for a malt. So what can I do for you, sir?

CALVADOS   It is a somewhat delicate matter.

CARRUTHERS   Delicate?

CALVADOS *(pause)* It concerns your colleague, Miss Riefenstahl.

CARRUTHERS   Yes. What about her?

CALVADOS   There have been, as you might say, some concerns, expressed in the Council about Miss Riefenstahl's presence in Valencia.

CARRUTHERS   I'm afraid you'll have to be a little more specific, Mr. Calvados.

CALVADOS   Her past.

CARRUTHERS What about her past?

CALVADOS   To be precise, about her close friendship with Adolf Hitler.

CARRUTHERS Well, I see what you mean, but there's only one word to respond to that, Mr. Calvados.

CALVADOS   Yes?

CARRUTHERS Guernica.

CALVADOS   Guernica?

CARRUTHERS Fifty German bombers blasted the town of Guernica out of existence, at the express request of your leader, General Franco, and courtesy of his Nazi friend, Adolf Hitler.

CALVADOS   Perhaps... but that was a long time ago.

CARRUTHERS No, not really, Mr. Calvados. It was 1936. Just about the same time as Miss Riefenstahl was making her films in Nazi Germany. And no one was killed in the making of them, I think that I can definitely vouch for that.

CALVADOS   That may indeed be so, sir, but nevertheless I am under considerable pressure from my colleagues to deport Miss Riefenstahl.

CARRUTHERS Deport her? On what possible grounds?

CALVADOS   It is very political, Mr. Carruthers, very political. I can say no more than that at this moment.

CARRUTHERS Mr. Calvados, let me tell you something which you may not know. Every time film critics draw up a list of the greatest films of all time, Miss Riefenstahl's documentaries come up somewhere at the top of that list. Every single time.

CALVADOS   Be that as it may, Mr. Carruthers...

CARRUTHERS But as Mr. Welles might say, no deal.

CALVADOS   As you say, no deal.

CARRUTHERS Mr. Calvados, there is ALWAYS a deal, it's just that we have to find out where it happens to be hiding.

Pause.

CALVADOS   Let me think about this for a moment. We do have a local Orphans Fund...

CARRUTHERS How much?

CALVADOS   Administered by my wife...

CARRUTHERS How much?

CALVADOS   Fifty English guineas.

CARRUTHERS Guineas, very English, Mr. Calvados. I will have the money with you the very first thing tomorrow morning, you have my word on it. Anything else?

CALVADOS   Only one matter, a rather delicate one. It concerns... it concerns Miss Rita Hayworth.

CARRUTHERS Who?

CALVADOS   Miss Hayworth. You know her?

CARRUTHERS No, not personally, but I believe that Mr. Welles was married to her for five years.

CALVADOS   A photograph of Miss Hayworth. *(Pause)* Signed — To Juanita.

CARRUTHERS Your wife?

CALVADOS   No. A close friend.

CARRUTHERS Then your close friend Juanita will have it in her sweet little hands within the month, Mr. Calvados.

CALVADOS   Thank you, Mr. Carruthers. *(As he leaves, he passes Leni at the door. He shakes her hand.)* Miss Riefenstahl, so pleased to meet you. I have always been a great admirer.

CARRUTHERS The Mayor, Mr. Calvados.

LENI   Nice to meet you.

He smiles and leaves.

LENI   Mr. Calvados, what is he doing here? Is there anything wrong?

CARRUTHERS No, Miss Riefenstahl, nothing wrong. Nothing in the world.

Scene 10

Diving sequence from Olympia on screen. Three days later. Leni is sitting with Orson in his room.

LENI   November, 1938. I was on top of the world. My film *Olympia*, it had won prizes all over Europe, even France. So off I went with it to your United States of America.

ORSON   Yes, I remember, I was there at your very first showing, in Chicago, up in the back row.

LENI   You were? Then why on earth didn't you come up and speak to me?

ORSON   Because I was in tears for most of the time, that's why. And me, go up and speak to the great Leni Riefenstahl? No, I was much too shy.

LENI   You, shy? I do not believe it, not for a single moment.

ORSON   It's true, Leni, I swear to you it's true. *Olympia* is the greatest sports film ever made. No one will ever make a better one. Hell, I have my own personal copy.

LENI   Counterfeit.

ORSON   Of course.

LENI   I have it with me.

ORSON   Then let the good times roll.

Torch sequence of Olympia on screen. Lights and Orson wipes his eyes.

ORSON   It always does that to me. Can't help it.

LENI   That means a great deal to me, Orson.

Silence.

ORSON   But what happened after that?

LENI   You know exactly what happened.

ORSON   Kristallnacht?

On the screen, stills of Kristallnacht.

LENI   No! No! It is not possible, this had nothing to do with the Führer. This is the propaganda of the enemies of Germany!

ORSON   And I seem to remember that, as of that exact moment, you received from the United States of America the Grand Order of Persona Non Grata.

LENI   Yes. Everything went sour for me in America from that moment on.

ORSON   But hold on — didn't you show *Olympia* to that old Fascist, Walt Disney?

LENI   Don't even speak to me about Walt Disney.

ORSON   They said that you slept with him.

LENI   Walt Disney?

ORSON   No, Adolf Hitler. In the States, they all said that you were Hitler's mistress.

LENI   No, never. The Führer, he wasn't really like that, at least not with me.

ORSON   But say, just say, that your Führer had put in a request, through formal channels, so to speak?

Pause.

LENI   Yes, of course I would have slept with him. Yes, but things would never have been the same.

ORSON   But you would have done it?

LENI   Yes. But as you Americans say, sex was at that time for me, no big deal.

ORSON   But think back, Leni, think right back to 1938. Kristallnacht — surely that was your big chance to break clear, to get out of Germany? *(Pause)* A whisper in the heart.

LENI   Orson, I swear to you, if there was ever such a whisper, then I never heard it.

ORSON   But surely you must have known what Hitler was doing to the Jews.

LENI   Yes and no. I was blind. We were all blind. In those days it was all about the Third Reich, the glorious future. It never once entered my head to leave Germany.

ORSON   But surely you knew?

LENI   Only some of it. But not about the camps, I swear to you. Not the camps.

ORSON   But just ignoring what was happening around you, that was all right?

LENI   Don't be self-righteous, Orson. It doesn't become you.

ORSON   Touché.

LENI   That was not the way I saw it at the time. Hitler. Back then, back in those days, Adolf Hitler, he was like a drug for me. Some terrible drug. *(She recovers herself)* But hold on, we've jumped four years. What about you?

ORSON   Let me think — yes, I got married — to a high society girl, Victoria Nicholson, a lovely woman, but much too good for someone like me. And I was getting into the Big Time, it was theatre in New York and radio, all for big bucks. Me, on radio, I was the Shadow.

LENI   The Shadow?

ORSON   Who knows what evil lurks in the hearts of men? The Shadow knows. *(A long, throaty cackle)* The Shadow strikes terror into all those sharpsters, lawbreakers and criminals who break the law. And he is brought to you tonight by Blue Coal, the coal that will provide a warm glow on winter nights. Tonight's episode is — the Circle of Death!

LENI   Remarkable, but hardly high art.

ORSON   No, but it sure paid the bills and, best of all, it gave me the cash to put into the real thing, the important stuff, my Harlem voodoo Macbeth.

LENI   Yes. I think that I heard something about that production.

ORSON   My black Macbeth, a guy called Jack Carter, he was an alcoholic, a great actor, but always five blocks away from his brains. Hell, Jack had done hard time for murder, he was as crazy as a waltzing mouse. One night he was right out of it and couldn't play, so I just went on and played Macbeth in his place.

LENI   But you were still working on radio.

ORSON   Yes, my radio work, that was what paid the bills for my black Macbeth, for all my stuff with Mercury Theatre. And then there was my big break-through.

Radio crackling/menacing music.

RADIO   "Carl Phillips here, CBS News. A huge flaming object has apparently dropped upon a farm in New Jersey — we will get back to you when we have further information". *(Jazz music)* "Wait a minute, someone's crawling. Someone... or something. I can see out of that black hole two luminous discs- are the eyes? It might be a face... it... Ladies and Gentlemen, it's indescribable. The eyes are black and gleam like a serpent. The mouth is V-shaped with saliva dripping from its rimless lips that seem to quiver and pulsate."

Orson laughs.

ORSON   1938, *War of the Worlds*. It caused chaos from New York to San Francisco. Hell, my friend John Barrymore, he let out all his dogs from their kennels and shouted to them: 'The world is ending, fend for yourselves!' *(Leni laughs.)* Oh, I got threatened with all manner of threats and lawsuits, but in the end it didn't amount to a row of beans. But whoop de doo, I was now the most famous radio actor on the planet — a thousand bucks a week.

LENI   You were rich.

ORSON   No, Leni, I was still dirt poor. Because I'd gone and pumped every dollar I had earned from radio into my Mercury Theatre and my Shakespeare production of *Five Kings*, three plays in one evening. And me, I was to play Falstaff. *(booms)* "Young men must live!" *(chuckles)* And you?

LENI   1939? War had been declared. So I went off to Poland as a war correspondent with all my crew. *(She stops and gulps.)* When we arrived in Cracow, our soldiers were lining up some Polish partisans. They simply shot them in the back without trial and dumped them into a lime pit. *(Pause)* No! No! In the name of God, what kind of soldiers are you?

OFFICER'S VOICE Someone shut that woman up. FIRE!

Sound of shots.

LENI   Next week, I made a point of visiting the Führer in Danzig and I reported to him in detail what had occurred the week before in Cracow.

ORSON   And he said that he would look into it?

LENI   Yes. And that was the last that I ever heard of it.

ORSON   Reality is a bitch, Leni.

LENI   I never thought of going back to newsreels. That was over.

ORSON   I don't blame you.

LENI   That must take us to 1940.

ORSON   Yes, the year that I divorced Virginia. Our relationship was never going to work. Hell, we only married so we could be together.

LENI   Oh, I thought that was the whole point of marriage.

ORSON   No, not for me. No, looking back I think that my main problem back in 1940 was calves.

LENI   Calves?

ORSON   Yes. I suddenly discovered that I had developed an unhealthy passion, an obsession, for the calves of ballerinas. This obsession, it only lasted for a few years then, just as suddenly, it vanished as if it had never been. Strange. But it was a crazy time for me then. Hollywood, RKO, was now hot on my trail, they offered me two and half grand a week and cakes — and best of all, final cut, complete control of my first movie.

LENI   Yes. The final cut. Complete control. Essential. But you haven't told me what happened to the Shakespeare play, *Five Kings*?

ORSON   Down the tubes, Leni, straight down the tubes. No, now I was going to make a movie of the novel *Heart of Darkness* for RKO. "The river is black tonight, my friends. It seems to look out, into a vast darkness". Those were to be the opening words of my movie. Wonderful, wonderful. *(Pause)* Had you now gone back to feature films?

LENI   Yes. I travelled off to Spain to make a feature film called *Tiefland*.

ORSON   Oh. I haven't seen that one, Leni.

LENI   No, it wasn't finished till well after the war.

ORSON   And it never reached us in the States.

LENI   It never will. But I have brought a copy with me. Would you like to take a look?

ORSON   Of course. Bring it up and I'll have a run through it tonight.

LENI   You will? Thank you, Orson, thank you.

Scene 11

Clip from the Pelota documentary.

NARRATOR   Scene 12 A week later. Leni and Carruthers view the Pelota documentary footage together.

CARRUTHERS This is excellent, and yesterday's work, his interviews with the little American boy are very good, very good indeed.

LENI   A very wise little boy.

CARRUTHERS Rather like Mr. Welles must have been, I should imagine.

LENI   Rather like he is now.

CARRUTHERS Indeed. You know, Miss Riefenstahl, I rather think that our little collaboration is turning out rather well. I must confess that I thought at the outset that Mr. Welles might find this type of project, shall we say...

LENI   Beneath him?

CARRUTHERS Frankly, yes. But he is a quite remarkable man, Mr. Welles. Many talents, but he bears them well.

LENI   Orson contains multitudes.

CARRUTHERS And his multitudes contain multitudes.

LENI   All battling for his attention.

CARRUTHERS And ours. *(Pause)* Miss Riefenstahl, I hope that you don't mind my asking you — are you enjoying our little project?

LENI   Immensely. Work has, as you might understand, been hard to come by in Germany in recent years. And I have always loved sport.

CARRUTHERS And I see that you have managed to spend some time with Mr. Welles.

LENI   Yes.

CARRUTHERS And to your mutual advantage, I trust?

LENI   I think so. We have, for the past fortnight, travelled erratically on what you might well describe as parallel chronological tracks.

CARRUTHERS I don't understand.

LENI We have been going through the story of our lives, and so far we have just about reached 1940.

CARRUTHERS Yes. 1940. The Blitz. Those were troubled times. *(He withdraws a piece of paper from his pocket, and hands it to her)* Has Mr. Welles mentioned this to you yet?

She slowly examines it, and scowls.

LENI No. Not yet.

CARRUTHERS But he undoubtedly will. Did you really mean all that you said here in this telegram?

LENI Yes, of course I did, at the time. Paris, 1940. Those were heady days for the Reich. Glorious days.

CARRUTHERS And did you ever regret sending it to Hitler?

LENI Yes, of course I did — every single day of my life since the war. But my telegram was not, by any standards, a war crime.

CARRUTHERS No. Of course not.

LENI Mr. Carruthers, I am now going to say to you something that I have never said before, and will probably never ever say again to anyone on earth. *(Pause)* Hitler's Germany was probably the world's first psychotic nation, I understand that now. And I played a part in that psychosis, even if I was blind to it at the time. But if I stood up and said that now, Germans would loathe me even more than they already do. Because I would drag them back and remind them of what they were. And that is the last thing in the world that they want to do.

CARRUTHERS But Miss Riefenstahl, you have never, at least not to my knowledge, ever publicly denounced Hitler.

LENI No, you are right, I haven't, and every single time that I try to do it, somehow, somehow the words seem to stick in my throat. I know that shouldn't happen, but it does. That man, Adolf Hitler, he is like a deep, dark disorder inside me... and I can't clear myself of it, however hard I try.

He stands and kisses her on the forehead.

CARRUTHERS I pity you, Miss Riefenstahl. I truly do.

Scene 12

Slides/film of Tiefland.

NARRATOR   Scene 13. Orson's room Orson is sitting at the table. Leni enters and sits down at the table with him.

Leni is visibly nervous.

LENI   My *Tiefland* film — have you managed to take a look at it?

ORSON   Yes, you could say that. I was up till two in the morning looking at it, Leni.

Leni withdraws an envelope from her handbag and lays it on the table.

LENI   Please don't open this envelope until I ask you to, Orson.

ORSON   Oh. Very mysterious, very mysterious indeed.

LENI   So?

ORSON   Leni, for the first time in many years I am labouring to combine tact with honesty.

LENI   No tact, please. Honesty will do.

ORSON   Your *Tiefland*. It's simply a silent movie with sound, Leni.

LENI   I see. You can open your envelope now, Orson.

He does so, and reads it aloud.

ORSON   "A silent movie with sound". Wow. I thought that I was supposed to be the magician here.

LENI   When you leave a film for years, and then you come back to it...

ORSON   It is fresh, almost as if you had never seen it before.

LENI   Exactly. You have established distance. You see it as it really is.

ORSON   But you were right, Leni. Kitsch with castanets, that's your *Tiefland*. The photography and the music, they are stunning, but this, this Leni, this is like something from the Dark Ages... the gypsy dancer, the cruel nobleman, the revolting peasants... give me a break, woman.

NARRATOR   Orson pours himself a drink and beckons to Leni, who nods. He pours her a drink. She sips it.

LENI   Orson, have you ever felt that your best work may well be behind you?

ORSON   I feel it every single day of my life, but I won't admit it, not even to myself.

LENI   And be honest with me Orson, is that what's happened to me?

ORSON   Leni, you made your *Tiefland* over ten years ago, and in those ten years you could have made a dozen movies, some good, some bad, some indifferent. That's how you grow, that's how you keep learning. But you haven't been given that precious time, Leni, and there's no getting away from that sad fact.

LENI   And let's be honest with each other, no one is ever going to give me another chance, Orson. I'm poison to any project.

ORSON   Movies, yes, but that doesn't mean that it's all over for you with a camera.

LENI   What do you mean?

ORSON   I mean that I've had a good look at some of the stills that you have taken here. They're just great, Leni, great.

LENI   You really think so?

ORSON   I KNOW so. So still photography, that could well be your next stop, Leni. Take a step back and take a long think about it.

LENI   I will, Orson, I will.

ORSON   Have a drink, woman. You may need it. *(He pours her a drink. He withdraws an envelope and hands it to her)* Here's an envelope from me now.

LENI   Oh.

ORSON   Please read it out loud, Leni.

LENI   "With indescribable joy, deeply moved and filled with burning gratitude, we share with you, my Führer, your and Germany's greatest victory, the entry of German troops into Paris. You exceed anything that human imagination has the power to conceive, achieving deeds without parallel in the history of mankind. How can we possibly thank you? To express congratulations is far too inadequate a way to convey to you the feelings that move me. Signed, your Leni Riefenstahl.

ORSON   Quite a mouthful, Leni.

LENI   We were drunk with power. Germany had conquered Poland, France, Holland...

ORSON   And you were at the very heart of it.

LENI   Yes, I was.

ORSON   And milking it for everything that you could get.

LENI   Yes, I was.

ORSON   But, looking back, was there anything that you would have done differently?

LENI   I could have fled to Switzerland or Sweden, but the fire inside me Orson, it was still burning too hot, too bright. Everything that I touched turned to gold — 1940 — and I was all primed to make *Penthilesea*, the story of the Amazon queen who fell in love with Achilles.

ORSON   And you would play Penthilsea?

LENI   Of course.

ORSON   Correct me if I'm wrong — this Amazon, doesn't she EAT Achilles at the finish?

LENI   Not quite. First, she tears him apart. Then she eats him, but it's all very symbolic.

ORSON   Tell that to Achilles. But that movie didn't come off?

LENI   No. The war. So I moved on to make *Tiefland*. Where are you now?

ORSON   In Hollywood. 1940. Like I told you, I was the Man of the Moment. RKO, they suddenly came up with big bucks to go out there and make a movie. But the money, that wasn't what was important, no, the important thing was that they were giving me complete control.

LENI   Yes. Complete control. Essential. And the film?

ORSON   Joseph Conrad's novel, *The Heart of Darkness*. But there was a problem. No one in the history of Hollywood had ever been given such a great deal. So suddenly, suddenly I was the most hated man in town. And the man who hated me most was a producer by the name of Harry Cohn.

COHN   Movies ain't art, movies are show business. But no, no, not for Wonder Boy Orson. His movies, his masterpieces, they had to change the world, perhaps even get Jews like me into the Hollywood Golf Club. Guys like Wilder and Hitchcock? They want you to ask yourself — what the hell happens next? Does the big mug get the girl, will the Sherriff beat the bad guy to the draw? Asses on seats, that's what movies are all about. But no, Wonder Boy Welles, he wants a million bucks to make something called *Heart of Darkness*, all about some nut-case holed up in the jungle. No, for him, movies are all about changing the way we see the world, changing the things we do. Well, I'll say it once and I won't say it again — no movie ever saved no Jew from Auschwitz.

LENI   So *Heart of Darkness* — did you ever make it?

ORSON   No, of course not — it was way too expensive, too big a jump. So I go off and write an original screenplay with Joe Mankiewicz. It was called *Citizen Kane*.

LENI   But you had never made a film before, you didn't know anything about how a camera worked.

ORSON   OK, so I high tail it to someone who DOES know — the top cameraman in Hollywood, Greg Toland.

Toland arrives.

TOLAND   Einstein, that was the first word that I said to Orson when we met, and he asked me to tell him all about cameras. Einstein said that any idiot could make things complicated, but it took a real genius to make them simple. So when Orson asked me how many weeks it would take me to explain it all to him, I said to him, forget about weeks, it'll take me half a day, because working behind a camera ain't rocket science. So then Orson quotes some goddam German at me: "des wissenschaft des nicht wissenwerten", he says. And I say to him, what in God's name is that? "the science of that which is not worth knowing." he answers, grinning all over his big mug. I knew exactly what he meant, because you get these guys who make a fancy living making a science out of everything from hitting a baseball to opening a can of beans. So I showed Orson how it all worked in an afternoon but on *Citizen Kane*, it was like I had never made a movie before.

ORSON   So I started work on *Kane*, with all the confidence of positive ignorance.

LENI   I could never have done that. No, with me, everything, every shot, had to be planned well in advance.

ORSON   Not with me. All the technical innovations that I made in *Citizen Kane* were possible because I didn't have the slightest idea of what was impossible. Hell, Leni, you did exactly the same in *Olympia* with your underwater shots — no one had ever done that before you.

LENI   Yes. That's true.

ORSON   Leni, sometimes you just have to jump out of the plane and build your wings on the way down. It's the only way. And that's exactly what I did in *Kane*.

Trailer for Citizen Kane.

LENI   *Citizen Kane.* It's a wonderful film.

ORSON   And I was dam' lucky to get it made. Because it was all touch and go for a while.

LENI   How?

ORSON   Our newspaper big-shot, Randolph Hearst, somehow he got it into his thick head that *Kane* was all about him.

LENI   And was it?

ORSON   If it was, Leni, then it was sure as hell at some deep subconscious level, I swear that to you on my mother's grave. Hearst, he tried to buy RKO out of it, but to their credit, the studio said no dice.

LENI   And the film was a great success.

ORSON   Yes and no. The critics loved *Kane* to bits. OK, so it made its money back, but *Kane* was no big smash at the box-office, at least not at the time.

LENI   So what came next?

ORSON   *The Magnificent Ambersons*, from a great book by Boothe Tarkington. You've seen it?

LENI *(pause)*   No... it was never released in Germany. The war.

ORSON   Well, it all went pretty well, and I finished it, and then before I had cut it, the President asked me to make a documentary for him down in Brazil.

LENI   President Roosevelt?

ORSON   Yes, I had been writing election speeches for FDR since back in 1940. A great man. The movie was political stuff, all aimed at promoting the American way of life in South America. *It's All True*, it was called.

LENI   Which means that it was a pack of lies. Propaganda, supporting fascist dictators.

ORSON   Yes, I suppose that's one way of putting it. Anyhow,

I high-tailed it down to Brazil, Rio de Janeiro, leaving the final editing of the *Ambersons* with RKO. But suddenly, there was a change of studio head, and some guy called Floyd Odlum took over.

Odlum arrives.

ODLUM   By the time that I had arrived at RKO, Orson was already down in Brazil, and he was balling broads like there was no tomorrow. He gets lost in Carnival and mambo and all that crap, then he goes and wastes weeks taking shots of fishermen, and doesn't use a foot of what he's taken. His crew are going crazy, cos most days Orson is balling away in some downtown brothel. And still there's nothing remotely resembling a shooting schedule. Soon we are down a million bucks, and still counting.

ORSON   While I was down in Brazil, RKO viewed the first edit of the *Ambersons*, but everyone at the studio hated it. Too downbeat, too pessimistic, they all said. So they decide to go off and shoot a completely different ending.

ODLUM   Then we had the *Ambersons*. The movie was too dam' long, and worst of all there was no happy ending — you've just gotta have a happy ending. That's show business.

LENI   So your film was ruined.

ORSON   Not ruined, but very badly damaged indeed. They threw a whole chunk of it out, and now those lost reels are probably gathering dust on a shelf somewhere in Santa Monica. Or they might have tossed them out into the Pacific, for all that I know.

LENI   Perhaps, perhaps some day you may find the ending to your film, Orson.

ORSON   Pigs might fly. *(Pause)* But let's get back to you.

LENI   I'm a few years ahead of you. I worked away throughout the war on *Tiefland*. Most of the time, I was struggling to find funding...

ORSON   Two per cent art and ninety eight per cent hustling. That's been the story of my life, Leni. The story of my life.

Scene 13

NARRATOR Next day, Orson's room. Carruthers enters, bearing a clip-board.

CARRUTHERS Broadcasting House has just reported back to me on the first reels of our first film, Mr. Welles.

ORSON You mean the rushes?

CARRUTHERS Rushes. Is that what they call them in Hollywood? Yes, the rushes. Excellent.

ORSON Your people back at the BBC, do they have any knowledge of Miss Riefenstahl's presence here in Valencia, Carruthers?

CARRUTHERS No. I saw no great need to inform the powers that be, Mr. Welles. I rather thought it best to consider this as a private arrangement.

ORSON Yes. A private arrangement. I think that I can see the title of a play there somewhere, Carruthers. Yes, I can just see it up there in lights in London, at Wyndham's Theatre. *A Private Arrangement,* a play by Orson Welles.

CARRUTHERS Possibly a sketch, sir. Or perhaps a revue.

ORSON So, where are we now on today's filming? The shoot of the big game with the top Catalans?

CARRUTHERS All is in accord, as they say. The stadium is booked, your players have just arrived, and they all appear to be in fine fettle. We film directly after lunch, which has been booked at a café close by.

ORSON I'm crazy about the Rioja here. So a bottle of the Rioja, por favour.

CARRUTHERS A flagon might be more appropriate, Mr. Welles, but no, not at lunch.

ORSON Well, have it your own way, Carruthers. And we are all set to get the film developed quickly, starting at five?

CARRUTHERS Yes, and editing can start after dinner, or tomorrow morning.

ORSON   And Miss Riefenstahl?

CARRUTHERS She spent most of yesterday afternoon filming two old priests playing pelota against a church wall.

ORSON   All afternoon?

CARRUTHERS Most of it, then she went on to take hundreds of photographs of the town square. Miss Riefenstahl is a very diligent lady indeed.

ORSON   Top banana.

CARRUTHERS Pardon?

ORSON   Top banana, a master of her craft.

CARRUTHERS Indeed, and she tells me that you have spent some time together, sharing anecdotes.

ORSON   That's one way of putting it, Carruthers, it's been a sort of long trail through our lives. Things that I hadn't thought about for years, if ever.

CARRUTHERS Most illuminating, I am sure.

ORSON   You can say that again.

CARRUTHERS The past is never really past. But yesterday she mentioned to me something that rather surprised me, Mr. Welles. She said that you had once written speeches for President Roosevelt.

ORSON   Yes, back in election year, 1940. Rabble-rousing stuff. Like your man Winston Churchill. You know the score.

CARRUTHERS Yes. But I venture to suggest that Miss Riefenstahl is possibly less acquainted with the vagaries of American politics than you are with their German equivalent.

ORSON   Yes, Carruthers. No question of that.

CARRUTHERS Then can I take it that she did not have to ask you about the boatload of Jewish children who were denied entry to the United States by your friend President Roosevelt in 1935?

ORSON   No. She didn't ask me about that.

CARRUTHERS Or that these Jewish children had to return to Germany, and that they all ended up in Auschwitz?

ORSON   No, I didn't know any of that either.

CARRUTHERS Or about Roosevelt's cutting the number of Jews at Harvard by eighty per cent, back in 1924 ?

ORSON   No.

CARRUTHERS And had you known about any of these matters would you have tried to bring them to the President's attention?

ORSON   No, Carruthers, I'm not sure that I would.

CARRUTHERS I see. You would, as we say in England, have sat on your hands.

ORSON   You have a quaint turn of phrase, Carruthers.

CARRUTHERS But surely you must have known about America's segregated regiments in the last war, Mr. Welles?

ORSON   Yes, everyone in the States knew about the black regiments.

CARRUTHERS And what did you say about them to the President?

ORSON   Nothing. It wasn't really my place to comment.

CARRUTHERS And in the Land of the Free, the Home of the Brave, exactly whose place might it have been, Mr. Welles?

Leni enters, carrying a big cardboard box.

CARRUTHERS I'll see to the preparations for the game, Mr. Welles.

ORSON   Yes. You just do that.

LENI   I somehow sense that you are not your normal sunny self, Orson.

CARRUTHERS Mr. Welles and I have just been discussing some rather arcane aspects of recent American history, Miss Riefenstahl.

LENI   Oh. Alas, that is not my area of knowledge, Mr. Carruthers.

CARRUTHERS No. That was the main reason for our discussion, Miss Riefenstahl.

He leaves.

LENI   We only have another couple of days, Orson. *(She hands him the box)* This is for you. Don't open it till tomorrow evening, under threat of death.

ORSON   Those are your strict orders?

LENI   Yes. Those are my strict orders. And I do hope that you will like what you see.

ORSON   Leni, you can't just leave me like this. Would you care to enlighten me on the contents?

LENI   No, I would not.

She is silent. He pours out two drinks, and hands one to her.

ORSON   We may well be reaching the end of the line, Leni. Where are we now?

LENI   1944. By that time I had married an officer, Lieutenant Jacob, and I brought him with me to the Bergkamp to meet with the Führer. Hitler stood with his back to us during the entire meeting.

Hitler appears.

HITLER   My generals, Miss Riefenstahl, my generals. No heart, no blood, not one of them. Stand your ground, I told them. Refuse to surrender, whatever the cost. *(Pause)* But no, they all gave in, they all fell apart. The Wehrmacht, my very best men, the cream of the crop. They should have stood firm and fought to the very last man. The Russians shot them, or sent them off to their gulags to die anyway. *(Pause)* Those Russians, they just kept coming at us in waves, Miss Riefenstahl. Why not, if they stopped for a moment, they were shot in the back by their Commissars. *(Pause)* Those Russians – how in God's name could they have built so many tanks.... so many tanks? *(Pause)* It is good to see you and your husband, Miss Riefenstahl. Goodbye.

ORSON   And that was it?

LENI   Yes, that was it. That was the last time I saw him. Thousands of men were still to die, but for the Führer the war was over.

ORSON   And what... what exactly did you feel at that moment?

LENI   Sadness. Sadness that such a great man could have fallen so low.

ORSON   But hold on, Leni — we're not talking *King Lear* here, we're talking *Richard the Third*.

LENI   I didn't know that at the time.

ORSON   But you know now.

LENI   I've told you, Hitler is in my blood, Orson, like some sort of ghastly virus. It is going to take me time to get that virus out of my system. If ever.

ORSON   So what happened after the war was over?

LENI   I fell into the hands of the Americans. A Lieutenant Schulberg, he was the first American to interview me.

SCHULBERG By the time that I interviewed her in the summer of 1945, the great Leni Riefenstahl was a quivering wreck. Her brother had been blown to bits, her father had died, her mother was desperately ill. She had lost all of her money and her home and every single print of her movies had vanished or been stolen. But she was lucky that it was Uncle Sam and not the Russkies that had got to her first. She had been sucking on the Nazi nipple for twelve years, getting anything that she wanted from her beloved Führer. And now, now it was all gone. Leni's little Nazi world had gone right down the tubes. But, looking back to those days, I got to say that I wish that I had got to know her better. I wish that I could have asked her the right questions, though I'm not sure that I would have got the right answers. But back then everything was so bitter, it was all about revenge. Because we had seen their camps, we had been to Dachau and Belsen, and by that time we were way, way beyond hate. So when you capture someone that close to Adolf Hitler, there's no way you can manage to be cool, calm and collected. No possible way. But, like most people who are fighting for their lives, Leni lied, she lied in her teeth, day after day. We knew that Hitler had built her a magnificent studio, but she said no, he hadn't. We knew that she had a direct line to her Führer's bunker, but she said no, that wasn't true. But looking back, had I been her, I would probably have done exactly the same thing. Lie till I dropped, fight for my life. And that was exactly what she did.

ORSON   Bud Schulberg. Did you know that he was the guy who kept you out of Hollywood back in 1938?

LENI   No, Orson, I didn't know that.

ORSON   And thus the whirligig of time brings its revenges.

LENI   I wish that I had stayed with your people; they certainly wanted me to. But I was captured by the French, and they grilled me for weeks.

Voices.

VOICE   Miss Riefenstahl, what was your reaction to Adolf Hitler's death?

LENI   I wept, I wept all night. What do you expect me to say?

VOICE   And what was your knowledge of the Nazi concentration camps?

LENI   They told me that the camps were for traitors, for enemies of the Reich. That was my understanding at the time.

VOICE   Would it surprise you to know, Miss Riefenstahl, that eight million Jews died in your Führer's camps?

LENI   No. That is an outright lie. That is quite impossible.

VOICE   I am now going to show you some film, Miss Riefenstahl, of what the Americans found when they entered Dachau.

Stills of Dachau.

LENI   No, no.

VOICE   Have some water, Miss Riefenstahl.

LENI   Thank you.

VOICE   So what do you think now of your precious Führer?

LENI   The Führer could have known nothing about this.

VOICE   Hitler knew, madam. He didn't write it down, but he sure as hell knew.

LENI *(weeping)* I can't go on, Orson. I can't go on.

ORSON   OK, so let me carry the ball for a bit, Leni. In 1943, I married Rita Hayworth. That marriage, it was another disaster. But I was still poison in Hollywood, so I went back to radio in New York, and wrote a political column for the *New York Times*. Anything to make a buck, Leni. My next movie, *The Stranger*, after the war, I played a Nazi war criminal hiding out in Hicksville. And I was one helluva Nazi, if I say so myself. Then back to the stage to direct a musical called *Round The World in Eighty Days*. Great special effects which didn't work and lousy songs. It did for musicals what Quasimodo did for coat-hangers. Then *The Lady From Shanghai*, with Rita, the weirdest great movie ever made, that's what the critics called it. That was in '47, a year before we got divorced. Then a Shakespeare movie, zero budget.

LENI   *Hamlet?*

ORSON   No. *Macbeth.*

Images of Macbeth.

ORSON   'Tomorrow, and tomorrow and tomorrow, creeps in this petty pace from day to day, to the last syllable of recorded time, And all our yesterdays have lighted fools the way to dusty death...'

LENI   'Out, out, brief candle, Life's but a walking shadow...'

ORSON   'A poor...'

LENI   'A poor player that struts and frets his hour upon the stage and then is heard no more.'

ORSON   'It is a tale, told by an idiot, full of sound and fury.'

LENI   'Signifying nothing.'

ORSON   OK, but let's not get too morbid, Leni.

LENI   We're closing in on NOW, Orson.

Zither music. Shot of shoes of Harry Lime, in shadows.

ORSON   Yes, 1949. *The Third Man*, with Carol Reed directing. Good man.

LENI   So?

ORSON   So what?

LENI   Give me the lines, Orson, the ones that everybody remembers.

ORSON   You mean the words that I put into the script myself, in that scene by the carnival wheel?

LENI   Yes. Of course.

ORSON   I'm not sure that I can still remember what I said. *(Pause)* 'You know what folks say about the Borgias, thirty years of terror and bloodshed, and yet they produce Michelangelo and the Sistine Chapel. While in Switzerland, they had five hundred years of democracy, peace and brotherly love, and what did they produce — the cuckoo clock!'

Leni laughs.

Scene 14

Orson's room. The final day. Carruthers enters, with a massive bottle of champagne and three glasses, to Orson and Leni at table. He pours out three glasses, and lifts his own.

CARRUTHERS I toast to the conclusion of what has been a most successful enterprise. Cheers.

LENI/ ORSON Cheers.

CARRUTHERS I know that both of you have spent many hours together recounting lives. But no, don't be troubled, but I would like to end your stay in Valencia with a few brief thoughts of my own. I began my working life with Lord Reith in the first years of the BBC, as a writer, but soon found that I had not the slightest talent in that discipline. I therefore resolved to be the means by which others, more talented than I, might succeed and prosper. And here in Valencia in 1955, what I have done, is to bring together, albeit for just a few brief moments, two of the greatest creative artists of the 20th century.

Leni and Orson raise their glasses.

LENI/ORSON Thank you.

CARRUTHERS I came to Valencia, Miss Riefenstahl, fully prepared to dislike you.

LENI   A little more than that.

CARRUTHERS Yes, possibly more than that. But strangely, our time together has driven me to cast my thoughts back to my times with Winston Churchill, when he came to speak at the BBC. And I thought to myself – did I ask him in 1926 why he had advised the gassing of rebellious Kurdish tribesmen? No, I did not. And in 1945, did I ask him why he had advocated having Mahatma Gandhi trodden under the feet of elephants? No, I did not. And did I ask why Dresden had been reduced to rubble and tens of thousands of innocent men, women and children burnt to death, to no possible strategic advantage? No, I did not. So no, Miss Riefenstahl, it would have been remarkable if you had refused to work for Adolf Hitler in Nazi Germany. Or that you Mr. Welles, would have protested about the thousand negroes who had been lynched since Franklin Delano Roosevelt had come into politics, or the millions who had been denied their democratic rights, their vote, for almost a century in the Home of the Brave, the Land of the Free.

ORSON   Touché.

CARRUTHERS Alas, both of you appear to be doomed. You, Mr. Welles, seem likely to spend the rest of your life drinking and whoring and acting in appalling productions in order to fund films which will rarely reach the silver screen. But all is not lost. By bending the knee to Hollywood and making a few potboilers you might also manage to make more *Citizen Kanes*. Mr. Welles, you must learn to grovel.

ORSON   I'll start tomorrow. You got any knee-pads?

CARRUTHERS And you, Miss Riefenstahl, whatever the merits of your case, you will always be stained by your connection with Adolf Hitler. But you still clearly possess an energy, and a visual genius, true genius, and you will never give up trying to express it, in some form or other. Never.

LENI   Thank you.

CARRUTHERS You see, artists like Orson Welles and Leni Riefenstahl won't die, won't ever leave us, no, you won't go anywhere simply because both of you will always be everywhere. *(Pause)* So, I raise my glass to you – both of you.

He lifts his glass, and drinks.

ORSON   Carruthers, I didn't really think you had it in you.

CARRUTHERS Neither did I. Rather a tour de force, if I say so myself.

LENI   Thank you for bringing me here to Valencia, Mr. Carruthers.

CARRUTHERS I must go now, and arrange for your taxi at the station for ten. I believe that you Miss Riefenstahl may have something to show Mr. Welles.

Leni rises and kisses him on the cheek. Carruthers is surprised, smiles, gathers himself and leaves.

ORSON   Well, I'll be damned.

LENI   For certain, Orson, for certain.

ORSON   But time's a-wasting. Do you have the slightest notion how to operate this Spanish projector?

LENI Of course I do. So if you would please put out the lights.

Orson puts out the lights. Darkness.

Clip of 'The Magnificent Ambersons'.

Darkness, and the light of the projector hits the wall. A flicker of the Ambersons, we see their rapt faces watching it then darkness.

Scene 15

NARRATOR Lights, as Leni switches them on.

ORSON Have you a handkerchief to hand, Leni? *(Leni offers him a handkerchief)* I've just got to blow my nose. *(He blows his nose, then dabs his eyes) The Magnificent Ambersons.* My lost final scenes. Haven't seen this film for over twelve years. How on earth did you ever lay hands on all this film, Leni?

LENI English actors and directors in Hollywood, sent them to Lord Reith. He passed the film on to Mr. Carruthers, who gave it to me for editing. I've been working on your film since the day after I arrived but there is another copy, so that you can make your own edit.

ORSON You've done a wonderful job, especially without a script.

LENI I have a confession. Mr. Carruthers, he took me for a private showing of the film at the cinema here. Otherwise an edit would have been rather difficult. Your *Ambersons*, it is just as good as *Kane*.

ORSON Thank you, Leni. That means a lot to me.

LENI And you were right. The Hollywood ending was weak.

ORSON The Happy Ending. Always leave them laughing. That's Hollywood, Leni.

LENI But life isn't always like that.

ORSON   You must know that better than anyone, Leni. No, my ending for the *Ambersons* was dark, very dark.

LENI   But right. Completely right.

ORSON   Maybe. But this must remain between us, Leni. No one else must ever see this ending. I want to keep this to myself.

LENI   I promise. *(Pause)* We have travelled quite a long way in two weeks, Orson, haven't we?

ORSON   Further than I could ever have imagined.

LENI   And our paths will never again cross, will they?

ORSON   Let's face it, it's highly unlikely I would ever be allowed to employ you on any of my movies, Leni. I'm having enough trouble as it is. No, you would be the kiss of death. So let me say this, before you go. I came here to Valencia fully expecting to meet Hitler's lying she-bitch, Leni Riefenstahl.

LENI   But you did, Orson, you did. And I came here to Spain to meet the selfish, all-engulfing Wunderkind Orson Welles.

ORSON   And you did, Leni, you found him, warts and all.

LENI   And have you forgiven me?

ORSON   Really nothing to forgive, Leni. But a helluva lot to understand.

LENI   The whisper in the heart.

ORSON   And while we are on the subject of hearts, have you found it in yours to forgive me, Leni?

LENI   Forgive you? What on earth for?

ORSON   For being such a profligate asshole, Leni. For messing up on the *Ambersons*, for not keeping my trap shut, for not going to Hollywood.

LENI   That's the past, another country. You will always squeeze the orange, always produce something of quality, even on a shoestring, half a shoestring.

ORSON   Even shoestrings might prove hard to come by, Leni. For someone like me. *(Silence. Orson stands and checks his watch)* Ten to ten. You'll be late for your train. Leni.

She rises slowly, walks round the table to him and kisses him on the mouth. She withdraws and looks him in the eyes.

LENI   There will be other trains.

Lights fade to blackout.

Darkness.

The end.

Tom McNab Plays

1986 *The Great Bunion Derby* broadcast on BBC Radio 4

1987 *The Strong Man* broadcast on BBC Radio 4

1992 *Winning* broadcast on BBC Radio 4

2004 *Houdini and Sir Arthur* rehearsed reading, Abbey Theatre St Albans

2005 *Dancing In The Dark* commissioned by ATTIC Theatre Company, premiered at Croydon Clocktower followed by a tour of venues in the London borough of Croydon.

2008 *1936* mounted by ATTIC Theatre Company as a staged radio play. Tara Arts Theatre, Croydon Clocktower and New Wimbledon Studio, London.

2010 *1936* The full production following script development premiered at Arcola Theatre in London and toured the South East of England.

2012 *1936* production re-mounted at the Lilian Baylis Theatre, Sadlers Wells to celebrate the 2012 London Olympics.

2014 *Leni-Leni* stage play about Leni Riefenstahl

2015 *Whisper in The Heart* Trestle Arts Base, staged rehearsed reading.

2017 *Leni-Leni* short film premiered in Berlin and was shown at Cannes Film Festival.

2017 *Orwell On Jura* Trestle Arts Base staged rehearsed reading.

NB *1936* is now titled *1936:Berlin*

Aurora Metro Books

some of our other plays and play collections

THREE PLAYS by Jonathan Moore
ISBN 978-0-9536757-2-2 £10.99

BLACK AND ASIAN PLAYS ANTHOLOGY introduced by Afia Nkrumah
ISBN 978-0-9536757-4-6 £12.99

PLAYS OF LOVE AND CONFLICT by Neil Duffield
ISBN 978-1-910798-79-9 £12.99

EASTERN PROMISE: Seven Plays from Central and Eastern Europe ed. Sian Evans
and Cheryl Robson
ISBN 978-0-9515877-9-9 £11.99

HARD TIMES adapted by Charles Way
ISBN 978-1-906582-48-7 £9.99

THE CURIOUS LIVES OF SHAKESPEARE AND CERVANTES by Asa Palomera
ISBN 978-1-911501-13-8 £9.99

THE UNDERGROUND MAN adapted by Nick Wood
ISBN 978-1-911501-10-7 £9.99

NEW SOUTH AFRICAN PLAYS ed. Charles J. Fourie
ISBN 978-0-9542330-1-3 £12.99

BIG THEATRE IN SMALL SPACES by Brendan Murray
ISBN 978-1-906582-18-0 £15.99

COLLECTOR OF TEARS and Other Monologues by Sean Burn
ISBN 978-1-906582-91-3 £8.99

PLAYS FOR TODAY BY WOMEN ed. Cheryl Robson and Rebecca Gillieron
ISBN 978-1-906582-11-1 £15.99

BALKAN PLOTS: New Plays from Central and Eastern Europe ed. Cheryl Robson
ISBN 978-0-9536757-3-9 £9.95

www.aurorametro.com

UK Ltd.